Contents

Acknowledgements

I wish to record my thanks to all the children whose words and pictures are included in this book.

My particular thanks must also go to:
Leone Burton, for the valuable advice she gave during the preparation and writing of the manuscript.
Neal Ascherson, for permission to quote from 'Tell the Children Wolfe Won Quebec' (The *Observer*, London, 26.7.87).
Roz Sullivan for the care she has taken in coping with my handwriting and the wordprocessor.
Brian Seagrove, Archivist, British and Foreign Schools Society, for giving permission to reprint the story of Robin Hood (Chapter 2).
Marion Casey, Basil Blackwell Ltd, for her ability in giving unity to a somewhat complex manuscript.
James Nash, Basil Blackwell Ltd, for his advice and encouragement.

Henry Pluckrose

"Regin smir" from Hylestad stavechurch is reproduced on the front cover by kind permission of the University Museum of National Antiquities, Oslo. (Photograph: Zodiaque)

National Curriculum documents are reproduced by permission of the Controller of Her Majesty's Stationary Office.

The study of history should be enjoyable in its own right and should lay the foundations not only for informed citizenship, but also for an enriched use of leisure time. A successful course in history ought to contribute towards the development of broadly-educated people who are effective in their various roles as citizens, parents and contributors to the common good.

History from 5 to 16
Curriculum Matters,
paragraph 58

The individual's knowledge of history, to be honest, is a rubbish-tip composed of ill-remembered lessons, what father did in the war, television documentaries with half the instalments missed, bodice-ripper historical novels, fragments of local folk-lore, the general idea of what that Frenchman seemed to be saying on the train, a dozen feature movies, what we saw of Edinburgh Castle before the wee boy got sick, several jokes about Henry VIII and that oil painting of the king lying dead on the battlefield with his face all green.

We all make ourselves out of the past, and find our own understanding of how we derive from it. Every child does it in a different way, and can be helped to do it better and more richly. In the teaching of history, it is that – not the curriculum – which is the core.

From 'Tell the Children
Wolfe won Quebec'
Neal Ascherson
writing in the *Observer* 26.7.87

Primary Matters: Editors' Preface

It is hard to find an acknowledgement of how recent are primary schools whose curriculum and management reflect the particular emotional, social, intellectual and physical needs of young children, nor of how far they have developed in a very brief time span. Indeed, there are teachers in today's primary schools who remember that in 1949, five years after the famous Butler Education Act, 36% of children of secondary age were still attending schools which also housed children under 11. Those same teachers have seen the development of primary schools through the Plowden era in the 1960s, the building of open-plan schools which aroused such intense international interest in the 1960s and '70s, into the 1980s and the new Act introducing a national curriculum and attainment targets for children of 7 and 11 years.

In the years following the First World War, successive government committees examined the educational needs of adolescents, of boys and girls in the middle years of childhood (7–11) and of children of 'infant and nursery' age. These committees reported between 1926 and 1933; their recommendations, though implemented in a piece-meal fashion, led to a considerable restructuring of schooling in England and Wales. The most profound effect of these changes was the acknowledgement that the primary years were a coherent and essential stage in the educational process, a stage which had distinctive needs and requirements. Prior to this, children had been educated in all-age schools. Unless a child were fortunate enough to be selected at the age of 11 (usually as a successful outcome of academic competition), the school s/he joined at 5 years of age would be the school s/he left at 13. Ninety per cent of the school population attended such schools and it became increasingly obvious that they were failing simultaneously to meet the differing needs of the 5-year-old, the child in the middle years, and of the 13-year-old school leaver. In the late 1930s, primary schools began to develop, with secondary (elementary) schools providing for those children who failed the selective examination. The distinctive categories of secondary education were enshrined in the 1944 Education Act which established a comprehensive tri-partite system of secondary education, but even five years later this was still not fully realised.

It took, therefore, some twenty years from the mid-1930s for primary schools to become generally established and, with the population explosion of the 1950s and '60s, primary school practice underwent many developments as the early years of schooling came to be regarded as an essential phase in the education process. Experiments were undertaken in teaching and learning methodology in the curriculum, in the organisation of classes (remember vertical or family grouping?), and, as already mentioned, in the architectural style of new schools. The curriculum became richer and more challenging to young children. Enthusiastic support for these changes was found in the report published by the Plowden Committee in 1967.

In contrast to this period, more recently primary education has been subject to critical appraisal and retrenchment. Academics (like Peters and Dearden) and politicians (like Boyson and Cox), as well as Inspectors from local education authorities and Her Majesty's Inspectorate, have focused attention upon the issues and assumptions underlying the work offered by teachers to young children. Are there things which *all* children should learn during their primary years? What constitutes essential knowledge for the primary-aged child? What should be the balance between the teaching of facts, the development of skills, the understanding of the concepts which underlie knowledge, and the processes through which this knowledge is acquired and developed? How effective are different classroom approaches in developing thinking skills, social awareness and responsibility? How can the primary curriculum best address the fundamental technological changes brought about by the microchip? In what ways are social issues such as racism, sexism or disadvantage best addressed? How should the particular insights and experiences of the disabled child be incorporated? How can institutional barriers to the involvement of all interested parties, especially parents, in the education of each child be dismantled? How should religious education be handled within a society which is more and more secular but also no longer made up of only one major faith group?

Questions such as these are not asked in a vacuum. They reflect the anxieties (real and imagined) of parents, academics, politicians, industrialists and, most of all, of the teachers themselves. That such questions are now being asked is, in part, a recognition of how far primary schools have come over the fifty or so years since they were first conceived. In a climate of concern and criticism, it is also easy to forget that British developments in primary education have been the focus of attention, respect and emulation in many other countries. Indeed, many have argued that it was a freedom from bureaucracy which gave English primary schools their unique character and made possible the kinds of thoughtful experiment which attracted an international reputation. At the same time, others have suggested that piecemeal development has led to idiosyncracy. Hence the current demand for every school to follow a programme reflecting clearly defined national criteria. However, the need for the individual teacher to make choices, ask questions, and influence every child's development continues to be respected and, however centralised the curriculum may become, however much the school programme is evaluated, however regularly children are tested against performance norms, the thoughtful teacher will continue to ask questions about *what* John or Akbar, Mary or Mai-Lin will learn, how they will learn it, what particular needs they have and how their individual interests, attitudes and aptitudes can be accommodated into the daily work of the classroom.

All the books in this series address aspects of these kinds of questions which teachers are asking as part of their concern to establish effective strategies for learning. Part of that concern focuses upon the links between the excitement of learning evidenced by young children, and the need to evaluate and maintain coherence in their experiences. Effective learning is the product of engagement as each and every member of the group struggles to make the learning process her or his own. At the same time, personal learning can still be limited unless it is placed in a broader context so that, for example, subject strands unite into a comprehensible and rational whole. Each author in this series seeks to indicate cross-curricular links, even though the titles indicate particular subject specialisms as starting points, so that the approach unifies rather than divides the child's experience of the curriculum.

As editors of this series, we wish to present to practising primary teachers a range of titles which recognises the complexity of the primary teacher's role. Each book will give shape and purpose to specific curriculum areas, dealing with issues which are particular to that specialism, presenting ideas for interesting and innovative practice in that area but, at the same time, emphasising the unity of the primary experience. Thus each title is set against a broad canvas, that of the primary school as a living and vibrant place in which young children grow and learn.

Leone Burton
Henry Pluckrose

1 History, its place and purpose

What was it like here before there was a me?

Jane, aged 4

In recent years the place which history should occupy within the curriculum of our schools has been the subject of fierce discussion. The debate has ranged over content (What shall we teach?), delivery (How shall we teach?) and even touched on the value of history as a unitary subject within the primary school curriculum (Could we not adopt an all-embracing 'humanities' approach?).

The debate has spawned countless documents, leaflets and articles in newspapers and journals. Some of these stress the need for a history curriculum which explores such issues as feminism, racism, colonialism, war and peace; some reflect upon the need to give children an understanding of their shared heritage and culture; others seem to suggest that since history is essentially narrative, a more simplistic 'then to now' approach provides an adequate sufficiency for young minds.

The discussion is, of course, more complex and wide-ranging than the simple summary outlined above. The answer to the question 'What should we teach our children about *the* past?' is bedevilled and confused with considerations which are as much political as educational. History comments upon values and attitudes and, in doing so, carries a message. The message might be clear and unequivocal: 'The Nazi regime in Germany in the 1930s was brutal and totalitarian'. Or it might be hidden: 'During the early years of the Second World War the Social Democratic Government of Sweden exported steel to Germany'. In reflecting on such statements we make a value judgement. For example the very juxtaposition of these two sentences might encourage the observation that Sweden, an avowedly neutral nation, co-operated with an evil regime and profited from war. It might also prompt the thought that the Swedish government could not have acted in any other way.

It is because history can lead the learner to reflect upon the values and attitudes adopted by society that its study is vulnerable to political interference. The story circulating in the Autumn of 1988, that many children in the Soviet Union were without history books because history was 'being rewritten' to take into account new views of Stalin, may be apocryphal. Yet it hints at the dangers inherent in the adoption of a history curriculum moulded to meet the requirements of the Government of the day.

The advent of modern technology has meant that the presentation of contemporary events can be even more controlled. Within days of the massacre in Tiananmen Square in 1989, China's 'old guard' were able to rewrite the past. People in the West saw television pictures of students confronting tanks. We listened as their leaders spoke of their hopes for the establishment of a less totalitarian regime. We mourned at the way in which their dreams were swept aside by armed force. Our perceptions of these events, and our response, ignored the political reality. Certainly the documentation of the happenings in the Square by the official Chinese News Agency – in which the soldiers were heros and the students were rabble – was very different from that offered by the Western media. Thus the record of events made available to the Chinese public was that which was acceptable *and useful* to those who held political power. This example from China should not be dismissed because it has been drawn from a totalitarian regime. The death of three members of the IRA on Gibraltar also illustrates how an event can be carefully edited to project a desired message.

These two examples indicate how careful we need to be when we present the past to children. The reign of Queen Victoria may have been characterised by thrift, dedication to work, self-help and religious observance. Yet these values – so admired by· some contemporary politicians – were advanced by a society which could tolerate child prostitution, the exploitation of women in factory and mine, poverty and a harsh penal code.

One way of helping to avoid the minefield of curriculum content is to accept that although there is a 'heartland of history' (to quote Roger Hennessey, HMI) schools should give children the opportunity to discover this heartland by providing them with the concepts and skills which are specific to the study of history. As the study of history is a recognised academic discipline it follows that it is a subject which can be explored in a particular and specialised way. If children are to study history and make some sense of it then they should be helped to realise 'what it is to be an historian', to examine the way an historian looks at material and interprets it.

Implicit in this approach is the belief that quite young children are able, at a level appropriate to their individual development, to grasp concepts and to develop skills which are peculiar to the study of history. As children develop an understanding of the nature of the historian's role, the need to prescribe 'the heartland' of the curriculum is diminished. Having developed an understanding of how to question the past, the skills so gained can be applied to any moment of the past (however recent or distant) and to any place, eg to a study of the village one lives in or to a study of the Egypt of the Pharaohs.

Chapter 2 examines in detail the skills and concepts which need to be learned in order to undertake an historical enquiry. Before that, however, it is necessary to try to establish the parameters within which the historian (young or old) will work. To do this we need to answer the question 'What is history?'

'What was it like here before there was a me?' *is* a historical question, profound and wide-ranging (Figure 1.1). History is an understanding of human actions *in the past*, an awareness of the human condition *in the past*, an appreciation of how human affairs have changed *through the past*, and a sensitivity to how men, women and children responded and lived through events *in the past*. The brief does not end there; if it did the historian would be little more than a voyeur in time. S/he is also concerned to find out 'not just what things were, but why things were what they were'[1].

This interest in humankind points, perhaps, to the reason why history as a subject merits an undisputed place in the curriculum of our primary schools. It is important for young children to be able to understand the present in the context of the past, to build upon their innate interest in 'what was'.

History seeks to grasp humankind. Herein lies the problem. So many men and women have lived through so many different periods of time, in so many different places, with so many different beliefs and attitudes and in so many contrasting cultures. To come to understand the nature of historical enquiry we perforce have to spotlight a small segment of the human past, to concentrate upon a particular period, place and people.

As the historian digs into the past s/he selects some materials, rejects others, assembling chosen fragments in an attempt to understand a time which can be entered only through the interpretation of evidence, the weighing of possibilities, the imaginative reconstruction of what might once have been.

This suggests that we should not begin to construct a curriculum for seven- to eleven-year-olds around a body of non-contentious historical 'facts' but around the development of skills which will enable children to study the past as enquirers capable of evaluating

Figure 1.1   *'What was it like here before there was a me?' A ten-year-old using a Victorian cemetery as a source of statistical information for a study of life expectancy in the 1880s.*

their chosen fragments in ways similar to those used by the professional historian. The difference in approach will be in degree rather than in direction for the stock of human experience and activity appropriate and available to children in their analyses is likely to be far more limited than that open to the adult.

From this it follows that the historian does not need to establish an agreed starting place; the past can be entered at any point and in any place. For teachers this presents a problem. To lead children into a study of history requires, of necessity, that some area of history be presented to them. For young children a study of their immediate past is more comprehensible than the study of a long-gone age where the differences between now and then are more marked than are its similarities. For older children almost any period can provide the opportunity to develop historical skills, although the more remote the time and place selected the more difficult it is likely to be to find evidence (documents, artefacts, buildings) that can be realistically questioned.

Thus an understanding of the nature of history does not depend upon predetermined and generally agreed points of entry or even of specific areas of study. History has no particular beginning in time and space and no particular end. It is infinite in its variety. History can embrace an epoch or an individual life, the study of a village or the study of a nation. Rather like a maze it has many entry points. To study history effectively it is necessary to make sure that the processes that are used are legitimate and meet accepted academic criteria. This point was stressed in the Final Report of The National Curriculum History Working Group.[2] To study history requires mastery of a particular and specific academic discipline (ordered 'enquiry, systematic analysis and evaluation, argument, logical rigour and a search for the truth'). If young people's minds are to be trained through disciplined study then they will also need to grasp something of the methods which are central to historical enquiry. 'Historians attempt to construct their own coherent accounts of the past by the rigorous testing of evidence which is often incomplete; the skills involved in doing this have benefited beyond the study of history.'

Accepting that it is possible to structure learning so that even young children can explore the past, is it imperative that they should do so? In many countries on the mainland of Europe history, as an academic subject, is not introduced to children in the primary years.

Some historical facts are presented through stories, projects and locally-based studies but the rigour which should accompany enquiry is often lacking.

The individual documents published by the Department of Education and Science lay the general foundations of the National Curriculum and set out the requirements of each. Integration across the disciplines which mark out the disciplines is encouraged but the skills needed to study each area are stressed.

The documents also emphasise the need to follow a curriculum which [...] throughout the years of [...] attention is given to the fashioning of [...] ordinary primary and middle stages of education and the secondary stage which follows them. Indeed it is in [...] history in each school will have a degree of commonality — commonality providing some uniformity across the age range, horizontally as well as vertically.

The commonality rests on the attainment targets (see Appendix) – achieved at levels appropriate to each child's age and ability; and on the four broad themes which underpin each historical topic which is studied (ie dimensions which have been defined as political; economic, technical and scientific; social and religious; cultural and aesthetic).

We have already examined some of the reasons for including history within the primary school curriculum. To these can be added others which stress the social and cultural dimensions which an understanding of history can bring. Like Jane (quoted at the beginning of this chapter) we all need to develop a personal sense of identity; to understand the subtle relationship between family, community and nation; to grasp the way in which local and national institutions have grown and developed; and to appreciate the beliefs which underpin the values and customs of the society into which we are born.

To these a further dimension can be added, that of cultural roots and shared heritage. Every child as s/he moves through school can be made aware of the inheritance s/he enjoys. Although not all the children in our schools will share the same religion or even mother tongue, all will benefit from an understanding of how the society in which they live has been shaped and developed over the centuries. An academically critical (ie not bland) approach to what has been called 'the British way of life' will better inform all who consider themselves to be members of minority groups (be these groups ones of language, religion, race, sex or class) as well as those who regard themselves as belonging to the social, political, religious, cultural or economic 'mainstream'.

Through the teaching of history it is possible to demonstrate and confirm that our national culture does not have one source but many; that our language and customs have not grown up in isolation, untouched by the global movements of peoples; that every society, if it is to survive, has to respond and adapt to elements over which it has no control. Although British heritage and culture derive from a complex past, a study of history will help place them within an understandable context. Hopefully it will also do more than this. A study of the roots of British society will help children appreciate the beliefs, cultures and social practices of other societies that they study – be these contemporary societies or ones which can only be explored through the eye of the historian.

To realise these goals presents a challenge. In many primary schools history is used, and appropriately so, as a vehicle for integrating the curriculum. Let me illustrate this with an example:

A group of five- and six-year-olds were studying 'water' as a topic. They had begun by listing things which float and things which sink (science). They explored the ways in which water could be contained and the shape of the containers they used. They asked mathematical questions 'Which holds the most?' 'Which holds the least?' 'How can we prove our findings to be true?' Informally the class teacher invited the children to discuss the way water is used in the home for washing and cooking (health), the shortage of water in some countries in the Third World (citizenship: geography), the water cycle (geography/science). In one of these informal 'talk' sessions Tom, aged six, remarked 'they didn't always have taps. My Nan (Grandmother) in Wales has a well. Did everyone use to have a drinking well?' The silence which followed was broken by Mary who lived in a tower block. 'But you couldn't have a well in a block of flats ... could you?' ...

The teacher seized the opportunity that this discussion provided to take the whole class on a walk around the block to look for evidence of domestic water points in the pavements and the hydrant points which the Fire Brigade use. A scale map of the walk was made (mathematics, geography). The teacher found another map which showed the route chosen by Hugh Myddleton, a 17th century engineer, who designed and constructed a waterway to bring fresh water from Hertfordshire into London. Since this route almost passed the school this map proved to be of considerable interest.

Here, in a project which embraced much spoken and written language, geography, science and mathematics (as well as art and environmental education), children had also been given the opportunity to question the past and to compare and contrast past and present. One must be aware, however, that if history is always buried in a basket of other subjects its particular distinctiveness *and the particular distinctiveness of the other subjects included in the topic* (each of which has its own specialist forms of enquiry) may, in consequence, be lost.

This is not to suggest that the topic or project approach is inappropriate for young children. Children tend to learn in a holistic rather than a subject-based framework; the project often provides an ideal method of presenting ideas in a meaningful form.

What is essential is that those teachers who follow a project approach ensure that the activities undertaken by the children develop what could be described as 'general skills' (book research, recording and representation in a variety of forms) as well as skills specific to individual academic disciplines.

Checklist: Teaching history

The following is an abridged checklist of the aims of teaching history. It has been compiled from a number of papers published since 1988 by the Department of Education and Science. They provide a context against which to evaluate the teaching and learning strategies suggested in the chapters which follow.

The aims of teaching history in schools are to enable children:

- to develop an interest in the past
- to understand the values of our society
- to learn about the major issues and events in their own country and of the world as well as the particularity of ordinary lives
- to develop a knowledge of chronology
- to understand how the past was different from the present and that people of other times and places may have had different values and attitudes from ours

- to understand the nature of evidence
- to distinguish between historical facts and their interpretation
- to look for explanations of change
- to understand that events have a multiplicity of causes
- to encourage understanding of the processes of change and continuity
- to develop insight . . . to obtain an informed appreciation . . . of the past

In addition it is hoped that the learning of history will contribute to the child's personal and social education by developing attitudes and values (such as respect for evidence, tolerance of a range of opinion) and encourage clear communication.

These aims are set against the objectives listed below.

By the age of 7 pupils should be able to:

- begin to understand that they themselves live in and are part of a country, a community and a world with their own heritages and histories;
- develop an understanding of their own and their families' past;
- begin to understand the concepts of 'past', 'present' and 'future';
- understand that evidence of the past comes in many forms;
- put objects or pictures with historical features in a sequence of 'before' or 'after' and give reasons for doing so;
- demonstrate that they know about some major and vivid events of the past;
- begin to distinguish between myths and legends about the past, and real events and real people;
- use basic vocabulary related to time such as: 'now', 'long ago', 'before', 'after';
- use imagination and evidence to describe life in past times;
- talk and begin to write clearly about these matters.

By the age of 11 pupils should be able to:

- demonstrate that they know of some major events of British and world history within a broad chronological structure;

- demonstrate that they have some understanding of the development of British society, and other societies, over long periods; illuminated by studies of shorter periods in greater depth;
- demonstrate that they appreciate the breadth and richness of history, for example by drawing attention to the technological, scientific and aesthetic achievements of the past as well as social and political developments;
- develop an understanding of the history of their immediate locality and relate this to wider themes;
- appreciate that different societies have held different beliefs, values and attitudes at different times and that the beliefs, values and attitudes of people in modern Britain have grown out of their past experiences;
- understand that evidence of the past may be interpreted in different ways;
- use chronological conventions (such as BC, AD, century) appropriately;
- make use of primary and secondary sources to support interpretations of historical events;
- make imaginative reconstructions of past situations which are in accord with available evidence;
- make simple causal connections, especially those involving historical characters and their actions;
- recognise similarities and differences between the past and the present day.

Reference

1   Carpenter, P *Teaching History – the ERA approach* 1964, p 31. Cambridge University Press

2 Concepts and skills

'We went to Hampton Court Palace, yesterday. At the main
gateway Concorde passed overhead.'

Michael, aged 8

As we have seen in the preceding chapter history makes a
multifaceted contribution to the primary school curriculum. One of
these facets is *knowledge* – information, understanding and content.
This knowledge comprises broadly agreed facts (eg dates, events,
places, the life spans of people) against which an historical
framework can be set, the relationship between accepted facts and
the evidence for them and the subject matter of a particular piece
of historical study. A second facet is the *appreciation* by the young
learner of the specific concepts which give history its status as an
academic discipline (eg chronology, sequencing, similarity and
change). The third, a facet which complements both of these,
consists of the *skills* implicit in all academic studies, the ability to
enquire from a range of sources, make judgments upon the
discoveries made and present them in such a form as to be
understood by another person (see Figure 2.1).

This suggests that teachers are presently able to offer to their
children a much more sophisticated approach to the learning of
history than has existed hitherto. I discovered the following piece of
writing in the archives of the British and Foreign Schools Society.
It was written by A Wright, aged nine, on 29 August, 1927. I include
it here as an example of a style of content and presentation which
is in complete contrast to that currently recommended by recent
HMI reports.

**The people of England were suffering from the tyranny of the
King and his nobles. In the year 1265 a battle was fought at
Evesham and the patriots were defeated. The survivors of the
battle were outlawed. Robin Hood was among them. He was
forced to flee for his life and sought refuge in the wild
Sherwood Forest in Nottinghamshire.**

It would probably be fair to assume that all the children in the class
copied the same lesson summary and that little or no attempt was
made by the teacher to develop in each young learner an historian's
approach to the past. That said, the idea that teachers should

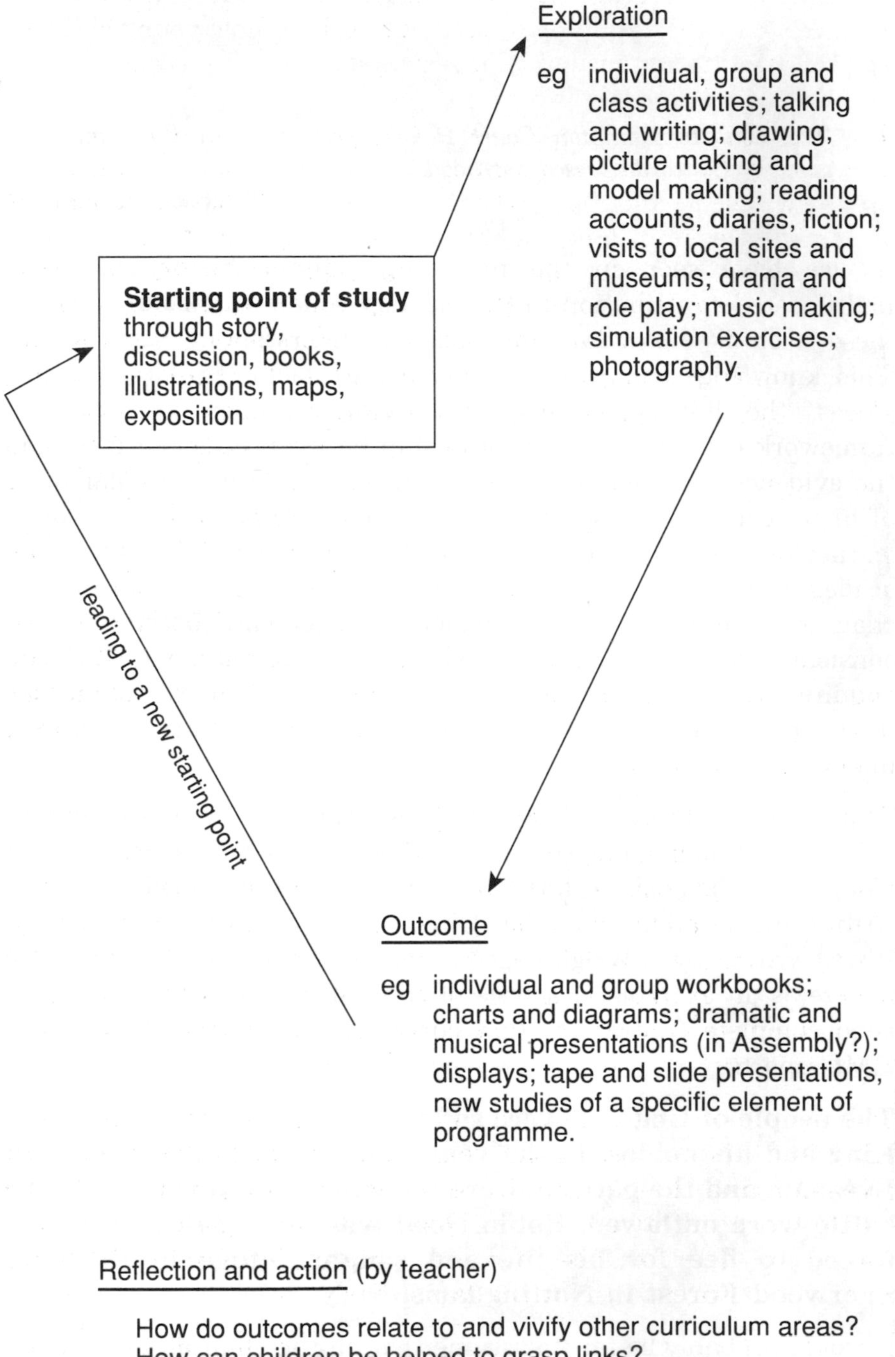

Exploration

eg   individual, group and
class activities; talking
and writing; drawing,
picture making and
model making; reading
accounts, diaries, fiction;
visits to local sites and
museums; drama and
role play; music making;
simulation exercises;
photography.

Starting point of study
through story,
discussion, books,
illustrations, maps,
exposition

leading to a new starting point

Outcome

eg   individual and group workbooks;
charts and diagrams; dramatic and
musical presentations (in Assembly?);
displays; tape and slide presentations,
new studies of a specific element of
programme.

Reflection and action (by teacher)

How do outcomes relate to and vivify other curriculum areas?
How can children be helped to grasp links?

Figure 2.1   *A diagram to illustrate the way in which a historical topic may
develop.*

concern themselves with the conceptual development of children is a comparatively recent one. To help appreciate the difficulties implicit in this expectation, let us consider briefly how young children acquire information, using as an example a visit to a zoo.

A zoo visit

The knowledge which our group of four-year-olds take with them to the zoo will be peculiar to each child and each will have acquired his or her knowledge in a personal way. John may have learned much from looking at books and talking about the pictures with his mother; Mary's information may have stemmed from her interest in her elder brother's collection of tame snakes. Zik might have learned much from TV, Siffra from listening to stories told her by her father about the Indian village in which he grew up.

The group have also listened to their teacher talking about the creatures they will see when they visit the zoo ... the elephant and the way it uses its trunk, the movement of the sealion through water, the swiftness of the gibbon through the trees.

Young children acquire information through a range of experiences, both haphazard and planned. If Concorde should pass over when the elephants are being studied it may well be Concorde's nose, rather than the elephant's trunk, which remains locked in the young learner's memory.

Of course the visit is likely to extend each child's understanding of animals. The sorts of questions which such an experience evokes are likely to stir the beginnings of some understanding of what thinking about animals involves. The experience might, for example, stimulate observations about the differences between one species and another, of meat eaters and grass eaters, of animals with long necks, and animals with thick coats. Basic classifications like these cannot come of themselves, unprovoked by some external stimulus.

Because understanding (or perception) is concept-dependent, communication about the world can only be expressed through a commonly-shared and agreed framework of concepts. In turn this framework provides a range of reference points within which to set any academic enquiry, even if that enquiry be at an elementary level. For example, the concept of the conservation of number gives meaning to mathematical processes – whether those processes are used by a six-year-old or by a University student.

Concept formation must be based upon personal experiences, for 'experiences without concepts are blind and concepts without

experiences are empty'[1]. Clarification of the concepts which underpin academic disciplines facilitates understanding and communication. Through clarification of the concepts we are able to separate
the various academic disciplines (or forms of thought). Once
concepts have been clearly defined and criteria established the
validity of a particular area of study can be evaluated.

Concepts and history

To study history, therefore, a young child should not simply be
offered a package of dates, events and quaint stories of the past,
enlivened with occasional periods of model making, painting and
drama. These activities may well fill a space in the school day, but
of themselves they do little to build up the concepts which are
central to an understanding of what it is to be an historian and to
enter the past.

It might be argued that the elements central to an understanding of
history are too abstract for a young child to grasp. A child with only
five years of life (and a considerably shorter period of remembered
living) is unlikely to have a 'concept of time' in any historical sense
(ie of a time which lies outside his own personal experience or
memory). Similarly, to suggest that children in the infant years can
be led to question historical 'evidence' would be foolhardy.

Yet even in the very young the seeds of specific historic concept
formation lie dormant, ready to be awakened. The five-year-old who
has heard her grandmother talk about her childhood and handled
her grandparents' 'treasures' is being made aware, albeit subtly, that
a time existed in which she, the child, had no place.

The concepts central to historical thinking – chronology, change and
continuity, cause and effect, the ability to weigh evidence and to be
sceptical and an empathy with people of time past – can be
developed from insignificant starting points. This cannot, however,
be left to chance.

Teaching implies intention, the intention that through the teacher's
activity children will develop as thinking, caring and responsible
people and acquire knowledge, concepts, ideas and skills in a range
of specified subject areas.

This implies that historical studies in the primary school should be
so designed as to develop and extend a child's understanding

through a variety of activities (see page 50) which will encourage a deepening awareness of the breadth of historical enquiry. At the same time they must provide opportunity for study in depth. This two-pronged approach will allow the teacher to develop the notion that the questions we might apply to a topic on the Egyptians are, in principle, the same as those which we might apply to the Victorians. It will provide children with the opportunity to dig deeply into a particular patch of the past and to use their growing skills to unravel it (see Chapters 7 and 9).

John Fines suggests that the sheer breadth of knowledge needed before any historical topic can be effectively studied bedevils history teaching in our schools. Nevertheless he is doubtful whether much is achieved by first insisting that children 'learn the knowledge' (ie facts). He writes

> we learn knowledge not by pitting ourselves against it, trying to learn by heart like an actor learning lines, but by learning it in action, in use ... we learn knowledge when it makes sense to us.[2]

Put another way, we possess knowledge when it becomes 'ours'; because it is 'ours' we have a personal relationship with it. The personal relationship makes the knowledge meaningful. Knowledge which is personally rooted in this way is not likely to vanish as soon as the lesson is over or when the moment of examination has passed.

Concepts checklist

History – specific concepts include:

- an appreciation of the importance of evidence, both primary (eg an artefact, a building) and secondary (eg a contemporary account of an event)
- an appreciation of chronology and sequencing
- an appreciation of cause
- a sense of empathy
- an appreciation of continuity and change
- the development of an historical imagination
- an awareness of the correct use of specific language used by historians. Taking examples from Key Stage 2 these would include such words as parliament, monarch, civil war,

labourer, conversion, settlement, invention, class, depression, conquest, manorial, network, inheritance, authority.

General skills which facilitate concept development include the ability:

- to uncover information through a variety of sources eg books, maps, pictures, diagrams, dioramas, objects, places, buildings, mathematical tables, conversation with older people (ie spoken comments about the remembered past).
- to observe, listen and record.
- to record in a variety of ways eg through the written word in all its forms; drawing, painting and photography; diagrams and charts; models.
- to communicate through personal recording, through speech, drama and movement.
- to translate information gained in one form and present it in another eg a pot seen in a museum described in words, an event in a book expressed through drama.
- to select, organise and present information, to test ideas.
- to recall information previously learned

Some concepts examined

When attempting to cater for children's conceptual development teachers face a most daunting task. A concept does not develop evenly, nor does it relate directly to age. The sections which follow therefore attempt to do little more than throw light upon the concepts peculiar to the academic study called history. Of course concepts are not directly taught as an exercise. Every history topic upon which a child, a group or a class embarks needs to be so shaped that the elements (and skills) which give validity to history as an academic study are stressed. Some of the strategies which are included can stand alone (eg *Milestones in my life* p 20). Others are best dealt with within the context of a specific topic (*Sequencing the day* (p 19), as part of a mathematics activity; *Sequencing pictures* (p 18), within a language lesson; *Family time lines* (p 24), as an element of a topic on family history).

Time, sequencing, change

If history is the 'study of man in time, the dead and the living'[3] and of events recorded and unrecorded, significant and obscure, then children, in coming to understand history, will need to be shown that it is also about change set within the framework of time. The concept of sequencing – of the ordering of historical events – is one of the most difficult for children to grasp.

Perhaps this is best illustrated by the number of books and schemes for primary schools which begin in the dim past and travel forward to our contemporary world. The sequence so often reflects the implicit attitude that immature and simple civilisations require little understanding but that of simple minds! Teach the seven-year-old about cave dwellers, his 11-year-old brother about man in space . . . Along with this goes the unspoken view that early peoples were simple and uncouth, that history is about ever-improving personal standards. The builders of Stonehenge might not have had *Dallas* or central heating, but they could think, construct and organise at a sophisticated level. Thus the programme we construct should seek to show how to sequence events without seeming to weigh the past against the present and, in doing so, finding the past wanting.

Sequencing illustrates an aspect of historical change. Another equally-important element is the gradual, almost unnoticed change which is implicit in all life. Historical change is a paradox. There is alteration and yet there is similarity and sameness.

Historical change is often slow and almost imperceptible. Care must be taken not to present history against too broad a time scale, which may over-dramatise change. For example, the development of the wheel is a popular topic in many schools, but the move from sledge and rollers to chariot, locomotive and motor car is often presented as a series of giant hops. Leaps through time may illustrate change by contrast: they do little to illustrate its nature. The young Richard II may be presented as a hero, but the heroic image fits him ill in later years. Yet young or old he remained that same Richard. This view of change is one which even children of infant age can understand. They themselves are now what they were not when they were born. They have changed; yet they are the same.*

Anne was looking at some photographs. 'That was me when I was a baby. That is me at the playgroup Christmas party. Would you know these (photographs) are me? I've grown up now.' Anne was six.

---

* Questions of 'change' and 'sameness' occur in many different academic disciplines and merit mention here. In rotating a shape (eg moving a triangle around an axis) we could ask 'What has changed? What is the same? What is different?' When multiplying a number by 10 or by 100 we could invite comment about the position of the digits and their past and present (ie after multiplication) place value. In exploring the properties of water we could encourage observations on the nature of steam, ice or condensation.

This little illustration serves as a useful introduction to the research work of John West. His study, based on primary schools in Dudley, set out to explore the ways in which children responded to historical material. To discover whether children could sequence, he presented them with material representative of a particular epoch (eg a drawing of a Stone Age tool, a painting of a Cavalier, a photograph of an Edwardian gentleman). The children were then asked to place the items in chronological order. Provided the examples used were not obscure (ie they fell within their likely interpretive ability) and were not too close in chronological time, the great majority of ten-year-olds were able to sequence effectively. The success rate fell dramatically when documents rather than artefacts/reproductions were used.

West's study drew upon 750 children aged between seven and 11. This group were not selected by IQ or social background. Because his study was to form the core of an academic dissertation on children's ability to think historically, they were given regular and sustained teaching which encouraged them to develop appropriate skills. West's research suggests that children of primary age are able to sequence. He also noted that 11-year-olds were able to use technical language with much greater facility than the control group. They were more aware that material presented as 'evidence' should never be accepted without questioning sources and motive.[4]

Children are not likely to grasp the idea of sequencing quickly. It is therefore important to set the period being studied within its broader historical context by regular references to the broadly-accepted historical periods (eg Stone Age, Saxon, Victorian etc). At the same time reference to sequencing can be made within the study of a specific historical topic. Oliver Cromwell, for example, lived during the same period as Charles I, yet he also outlived him. Samuel Pepys was a contemporary of Cromwell but saw the Restoration of the monarchy and survived the Plague of 1665 and the Great Fire of London of 1666.

Classroom timelines could be used to show both the broad sequence of history and the more subtle changes which occur over shorter periods of time. Drawings of Charles I, Cromwell and Pepys might be grouped together on the broad timeline as people who were alive in the Stuart period; they could also be arranged on the period time line against year of birth or death to give a much more finely tuned sequential pattern. If such a broad and tightly focused approach is adopted, one wide-ranging historical timeline could be displayed throughout the school year with mini-timelines constructed for each individual project or topic covered.

Strategies – sequencing

1 Discuss the order in which one does a simple activity eg getting dressed, having a bath, making a sandwich, using a calculator to resolve $7 \times 6 - 3$, buying a cake. Explore ways of presenting this activity orally, in writing, pictorially and diagrammatically.
2 Sequence the school day.
3 Sequence each child's day. How do these individual sequence statements fit into **2** above?
4 Play a sequence 'game': provide a collection of photographs of people, artefacts, machines, buildings. These should represent different historical epochs eg Roman, Saxon, Norman, Tudor, Georgian, Victorian, contemporary. Initially allow the group to try to sequence within particular subject sets eg clothing, weapons, ships, houses etc. When the group are reasonably efficient in sequencing these sub-sets, mix them to give greater complexity to the activity.
5 Following upon sessions based on local studies (see Chapter 3) explore the area immediately around school and encourage children to date and sequence particular buildings. These can then be drawn and sequenced on a timeline (see Figure 2.6).
6 Display three (or more) pictures which relate to each other in some way, eg Picture 1: A mother greeting her children; Picture 2: a house in a wood; Picture 3: the children alone on a dark forest path.

Construct a simple story from these pictures. Now discuss how by changing the sequence a different story emerges. Using the example above, how does the story change if the pictures are sequenced 3, 2, 1 rather than 2, 1, 3? Encourage children to make their own set of pictures to explore sequence variations.

Historical time

Change is set within the context of historical time. Jacqueline's comments about the memorable happenings in her short life (see Figure 2.2) are presented against conventional calendar time. The

```
All about me, by Jacqueline

My age

0           I was born on 23rd April 1981 at 3.00 in the morning.
1           I weighed 6 lbs 4 ozs.  I was born in Exeter General
            Hospital.
1           My mum and dad moved from St. David's, Exeter, in October
            1982.
2           They came to St. Austel. I came too.
2           My sister Ruth was born on June 7th 1983.  She had red
3           hair and my old pram.
3           My grandpa Blake died.
            He was very old (78).
            I did not go to the funeral.
4           I don't remember him very well.
4           I joined the playgroup in the village hall.
            I cried when I first joined.
5           But I did like it.
5           I started school.
            I broke my arm on the first day.
6           I fell over in the playground.
6           When I was in Mrs Smith's class we went to Home Lea Farm.
            They had some horses there.
            We all rode in the farmer's big cart.
7           It was last summer, July 1987.
7           I am now seven years old.
            I had my birthday in April.
            I was given a rabbit and a hutch to keep her in.
            She is called Floppy.
```

Figure 2.2   *Milestones in my life.*

children had been invited to record 'milestones' in their lives. To do so with accuracy, each child had to consult 'experts' on the past (ie their mothers and fathers). This calendar-bound time is not necessarily the kind of time in which children live and grow. For young children, the idea of time is personal, and in our adult terms it may seem insecure and shapeless. But because a child's sense of time is not the same as our sense of time (ie verbalised and packaged into years, months, days, hours and minutes) it does not follow that children have no *time sense*. Their time is not the time of the digital watch but time which responds and echoes to the ebb and flow of their everyday life. When something exciting is about to happen, time drags. When the event has happened (eg Christmas Day), it is often consigned to the dustbin of yesterday.

Joan Blyth, in a small-scale study which she undertook with a group of five- and six-year-olds, concluded that they had some understanding of 'oldness' – classifying time in the divisions very, very old; old; not old. She noted that 'old' came to mean different things to each of the six children who used it ... but 'something to all of them'. She also noted that dates were meaningless unless they were personally related to the individual child.[5]

This reflects my own observations of children and time. Before children come to school, time in the conventional calendar sense impinges very little upon their consciousness. For them, time is very much more relaxed, even poetical.

> *Days come.*
> *They wake us,*
> *time and time over.*
> *Where can we live but days?**

Although young children may be unable to grasp the fixed divisions of clock time or the ordered date line which stretches back into the past, it would be false to assume that in each school age group all children have an equally undeveloped time sense. Whilst work with young children might well concentrate upon the immediacies of daily life, some children will also be able to grasp time at a more profound level.

David, aged six, after a period of several weeks studying flight, observed 'My Grandma was born in 1903. That's the same year as the Wright brothers first flew. My Grandma is still alive. All air travel from Wright to Concorde has happened in her life.' Terence,

* From 'Days' by Philip Larkin, in *Collected Works* (Faber and Faber, 1988)

also six, was upset that a close family friend had suddenly died at the age of 35. He remarked that his mother was the same age.

Anna, aged nine, was linguistically less fluent than David. But her remarks on buying a medieval tile at an excavation site also point to a feeling for time past related to time present. She chose a cracked biscuit faced tile rather than a prettier glazed one. On being asked why she had chosen as she had, she replied, 'This one has a very, very dead dog's paw mark in the clay.' 'Very, very dead?' I asked. 'Yes. Dead means like now. Very dead means years ago. Very very dead is so far ago you can't imagine.' (Notice the use of the word 'far' rather than the word 'long'.)

Seduced by the neatness of chronology, successive generations of teachers have educated successive generations of children to regard history as an exercise in date hopping. Yet very young children do not need chronology to experience history. They need only to conceive of an event as having happened in the past ... or, put another way, to see the past as complementary to the present.*

This is not to avoid facing issues which are central to an understanding of history – issues like sequence and change. With five- and six-year-olds, one needs to confront the past within the present and, perhaps, the present as past in the future! 'Once upon a time ... Long, long ago ... One day, before you were born ...' now ... yesterday ... not now ... tomorrow' *may* lead to questions on the differences between now and then, of time and place. But even if the story only helps establish that 'now' and 'then' have similarities and differences its purpose will have been achieved. To take children back into a world in which 'was' becomes 'is', in which they can identify with characters in terms of 'now' (with each character having an unknown future) provides an experience which can play a crucial part in the development of their thinking (and ultimately their understanding of history). Within almost any story chosen for young children, the characters will have an identification with their own fictional or legendary past. For the children looking in on the action, time is suspended. On an adult level perhaps this is what the French historian Braudel means when he suggests that historians need the ability to 'become displaced in an unfamiliar past'.[6]

*Time present and time past
Are both perhaps present in time future
And time future contained in time past
(Lines 1–3, 'Burnt Norton' *Four Quartets* by T S Eliot)

Personal observations of children would suggest that we have become trapped into assuming that because it is difficult for children to grasp the time-ordered adult world, time has little meaning for children. If, however, we define time in the sense that young children use it, ie 'any time before now' we can use this as a base on which to build an understanding of the dimension and spread of historical time. West (quoted above) takes a similar view. It is said that 'children have no concept of time – yet the same children cope with equally baffling and complex concepts in other areas of the curriculum'.[4] This view is supported by the HMI booklet on approaches to the teaching of history.

It may be more helpful to concentrate less on historical time and more on an understanding of historical chronology ... The ability to conceive the duration of historical time and of the difference, for example, between 500 years and 2000 years is difficult for the young but for most adults too.[7]

In a report published in 1963, Gustav Jahoda suggests that children under the age of nine lack time perspective.

It is shallow, becoming nebulous beyond the span of one or two generations ... at about the age of 11 they begin to develop the concept of historical time[8]

This view is confirmed by West[4] who observed that even at the age of 11 children still tended to reason in concrete operational terms (ie the Piagetian stage which precedes formal abstract thinking).

None of this means that the idea of chronology cannot be introduced or understood. Children will need to acquire sign posts to begin to appreciate sequence and slowly to absorb such reference points as will allow them to gain some understanding of their own position in time.

West concludes that children's difficulties in understanding stem from two main causes. First, children lack basic vocabulary. Therefore it needs to be taught. This point is made with great force in *History in the Primary and Secondary years – an HMI view.*

History involves an ability to see the meanings and implications of language ... The study of history contributes to the development of language. The more confident and sensitive use of language can make pupils better historians.[7]

Second, (West suggests) the concepts which underpin the language are often mathematical and only partly understood. This means that we should not leave concept development and its related language to chance.[4] However we organise our timetable (integrated studies within an integrated day or formal subject-centred lessons) we cannot ignore the implications.

Strategies for 'time'

Mount a timeline around the classroom.

1 For young children (5–7) the line could relate to the more immediate past, indicating the year in which the majority of the class group were born and the likely position of the birth years of their parents and grandparents (see Figure 2.3). Such a chart could be supported with family photographs or children's drawings.

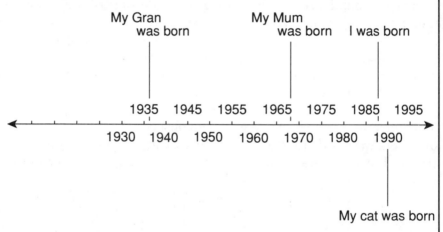

Figure 2.3 *Personal timeline*

2 For children in years 4–6 the timeline can take in a broader spread of time, indicating the principal epochs of English, Welsh or Scottish history, ie pre-Roman, Roman, Saxon, Norman, Medieval, Tudor, Stuart, Georgian, Victorian, Edwardian, contemporary. The line must be displayed in such a fashion that it can be referred to whenever it is appropriate to do so. (For example, in the form of an attractive frieze along the wall of the classroom.) It is useful if the chart can be regarded as 'consumable', with information being added by teacher and children throughout the

year. Apart from 'O' (the idea of BC/AD) dates are not too important, though those which continually recur and act as markers (eg 1066, 1815, 1914) should be recorded, the children choosing their own 'markers'. The impact of the chart should lead children to an appreciation of the *scale* of time past. This can be achieved by displaying a personal time scale within and against the large chart.

3   Each child could construct their own time chart of English, Welsh or local history. This would record things which are of personal interest to the child; these could be wide-ranging (eg events) or specific (the changing shape of costume, house styles, armour and weapons, ships).

4   The presentation and study of time has obvious links with topic work in mathematics. How can we express an abstract idea (like time) within a graphic, pictorial or written form? Figures 2.4–2.6 show different forms of time chart, based on a study of St Peter's Church and the buildings around it. Thus the construction of timelines could be regarded as a mathematically (rather than historically) based activity.

5   *Imagining*: invite the children to comment on and discuss the following:

   • *If you were selecting things that you possess to have with you for all time what would you choose? What would these choices tell people living in the future about you?*
   • *If you were burying some things to tell future archaeologists about your school what things would you put into your time capsule and why?*
   • *If you could choose one modern building in your town to stand for the next 2000 years which building would you choose and why? What would it tell people about our society?*

6   Make time boxes for the children. Collect objects or pictures which range from past to present. Sort them into shoe boxes. The contents of each box could reflect particular ways of thinking about time:

   • *Epoch*   eg Victorian to contemporary. The contents of such a box might include a Victorian penny, a ginger beer bottle, a George VI stamp, an army badge, a 78 rpm gramophone record, a photograph of a Spitfire, a three-

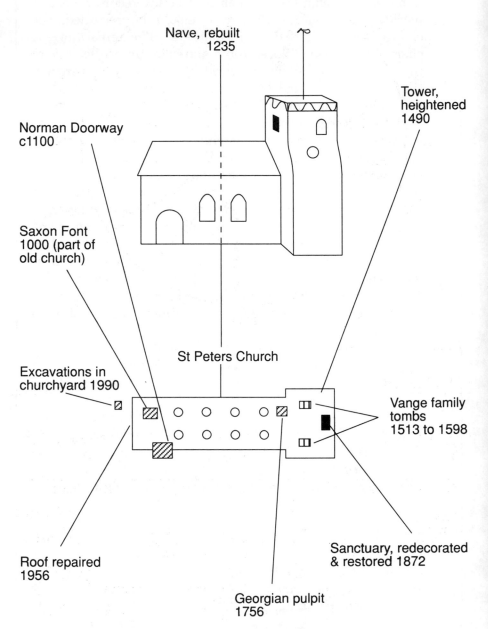

Nave, rebuilt
1235

Tower,
heightened
1490

Norman Doorway
c1100

Saxon Font
1000 (part of
old church)

St Peters Church

Excavations in
churchyard 1990

Vange family
tombs
1513 to 1598

Roof repaired
1956

Sanctuary, redecorated
& restored 1872

Georgian pulpit
1756

Figure 2.4   *A timechart*   Using an historic building to show change over
time.

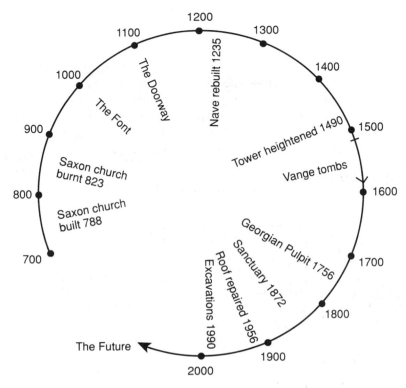

Figure 2.5 *A circular timechart, St Peter's church.*

The Church

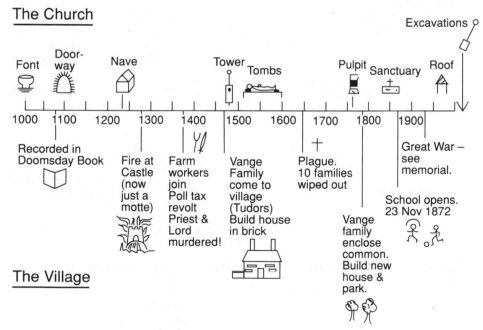

Figure 2.6 *A linear timechart.*

penny piece, a pair of scissors made from plastic, a football rosette.

- *Materials* ie how materials have changed in use over time. This is a more difficult box to prepare. It could contain objects made principally of one material (eg glass/metal/paper/stone/plastic/wood/clay/leather/ bone/fabric) or of a range of objects which, though made in different materials, give hints about their use and age. The contents of such a box might include a Ration Book or Identity card, a fossil, a Victorian brooch, a glass bottle stop, a candle snuffer, an old craft tool (eg a lace maker's hook), a two-pin electric plug, a large iron door key, a photograph taken in the 1920s, a quill pen, a scrap of carved or incised stone or wood.

- *Style* ie how design has changed over time. This can be presented through pictures. The box could contain pictures and photographs of a Roman fort, a Saxon church, a Norman castle, a Medieval manor, a Tudor house, a Jacobean manor, a Georgian mansion, a Victorian factory, a nuclear power station, a supermarket and a 1930s garage forecourt.

- *Technology* This box is similar to that described above. It could contain pictures of a range of everyday objects which reflect technological change, eg a flint axe head, a medieval knife, a Roman comb, two kinds of tin opener (handblade, hand or wall mounted wheel) a penny farthing bike, a 1900s car, a besom broom, a modern vacuum cleaner, a coal hearth and oven, a microwave oven, a 1930s radio, a 1990s stereo-bank, early coinage, a credit card.

Encourage the children to examine the contents of the box and then group and order the contents, justifying the order they choose.

Historical empathy

Historical empathy is the ability to enter into some informed appreciation of the predicaments or points of view of other people in the past. It depends upon an imaginative interpretation of evidence and on an ability to be aware of anachronism.[9]

Superficially it might appear easy for young children, rich in fantasy, to enter a past age. In a book published in 1959, R J Unstead, an enthusiastic primary school headteacher and writer, described how the fantasy world of children could be used as a means of taking children into the past. He wrote:

> A child's lack of experience and preconceived ideas is an asset for he can enter into the life of the lake village or manor with the same ease and gusto that permits him to transform a collection of old tins and planks into an Indian encampment.[10]

Empathy requires more than tins and planks. Historical sensitivity is more than child's play. It requires that the living perceive and understand things in the way in which they were perceived and understood by those long dead. The appearance of Halley's comet is greeted by modern scientists with enthusiasm. To the Saxon it brought fear and foreboding. Because Alfred burned some cakes it does not follow that a seven-year-old, when told the story, will be able to empathise with him because burning cakes is comprehensible *to her*. If Alfred *did* burn cakes the story comments more upon his state of mind than that of his ability as a cook – sophistications that a seven-year-old will find hard to share.

The French historian Marc Bloch questions the level to which we can empathise with the past. Because children know what it is to be human, they are able to relate their humanity to another's. Yet, asks Bloch, can I as an individual *really* do this without first having had a similar experience myself? After the fall of France in 1940 he wrote:

> Defeat. Did I truly know in the full sense of that word, did I *know* what it meant for an army to be crushed, what it meant for a people to meet defeat? In the last analysis it is by borrowing from our daily experiences and by shading them with new tints that we derive the elements which help us to restore the past.[11]

The ability for anyone to empathise will be governed by their own experiences, real or vicarious. Observe five-year-olds watching a play. Their whole bodies seem to speak of their participation. A witch appears, taking two children into her power. The audience sympathise and share the young actors' fear and anxiety. Released from her spell, like the actors, the onlookers relax and laugh. The tension has gone.

This seemingly innate ability to respond to the dilemma of the human condition is reflected in many ways. Few adults can watch

King Lear and not be emotionally stirred, read the last chapter of
Mill on the Floss and not be moved, watch bone-thin children from
the Sudan limp wearily across the TV screen and not feel pity and
compassion.

This suggests that children may be able to relate to people who lived
in another time and in another place when they are shown to have
had a human dimension. These people of the past ate, dressed,
played, decorated themselves with ornaments, quarrelled, married,
built homes, told stories, worshipped gods, made music, raised
children, died ... strands of life which are comprehensible across
time because they are timeless. This said, we should take care not
to distort the human dimension. We might, for example, invite a
ten-year-old to imagine what it might have been like to have worked
on a cotton plantation in a Southern State in the Americas in the
early 1800s. We may be impressed at the resulting piece of work
which includes an impassioned rebuttal of slavery and a demand for
negro emancipation. Yet such a response will perforce be contrived,
for even the most sophisticated and mature find it difficult to avoid
stereotyping when they venture beyond the confines of the time and
space of their own cultural base.

Within these restraints, however, young children should be encouraged to empathise with people of time past, to imagine what it
might have been like to be a Victorian chimney sweep or a Royalist
hidden from a Roundhead troop. Inability to empathise should not
be taken as a measure of a child's historical failure, although the gift
to relive, through imagination, actions and events of a past age
certainly provides a valuable starting point for understanding.

In effect, empathy is a reconstruction exercise, based upon sources
which are not far from the individual child's own level of perceptual
development. A six-year-old can handle a Stone Age flint and in
chipping its sharp edge against a sliver of wood get some
understanding of how it may once have been used. At a higher level,
empathy requires the child to put himself in another's place. It is
something which many children can do. Ralph, aged nine, came
from a reasonably prosperous middle-class family. He visited
Oxburgh Hall (Norfolk). Whilst there he saw the priest's holes and
learned a little about the struggle between King Charles and
Parliament and of the religious divisions within his Kingdom. That
night he wrote the following in his school journey diary:

At home in 1640
I watched the wood fire crackle and flicker and the candle

melt away. The wind was howling and beating against the
shutter. I walked to the fire place where the flames leapt up the
big chimney. I poured out the ale. I drained it, listening to
Father talking about Cromwell. 'Up to bed now' said Mother.
I kissed my parents good night and climbed the big staircase to
my room. Before huddling beneath the covers I peered out of
the window. The soldier was still on guard!

On a lighter, but still personal level, Alice aged eight, was taken with
her class to Chilham Castle (Kent) where the owner and his wife
attempt to reconstruct history by dressing as medieval characters
for organised school parties.

Returning to school, she decided to present her experience as though
she were a medieval child. Her writing style attempted to capture
the flavour of the period and was obviously influenced by the books
she had read:

Upon the scene there came to greet us fair Lady Joan, all
garbed black velvet and silk. She said to us that her Knight
would come to show us deeds of strength and courage. Upon
that she led us, jewels sparkling, to the loo . . . The Knight, her
husband, appeared and he was very old. His name, he said, was
'Knight of the black gauntlet' and his gallant steed was Regent.
Then the quintain he did charge . . . He hit it and it swirled
round and did pain him on the back. He did it again and again.
Then we were left to the lady's care . . .
(After lunch) Across the formal gardens swiftly went a man.
Upon his wrist, a falcon perched . . .
We left by the latest invention, train.

If we use Lee and Ashby's classification of empathy level* based
upon their teaching and observations at Bramston School in Essex,
Alice and Ralph have been able to project themselves into the
situation 'to state what it would be like for me to have been there'[12]
ie reaching level 3.

Not all children of nine and ten are able to reflect in this way.
Indeed Ashby and Lee's paper suggests that some children in

* Five levels are identified 1 Divi past – inability of pupil to 'envisage complexity of human
institutions and interactions'. 2 Generalised stereotypes – inability of pupil 'to distinguish
what people now know and think from what people in past knew and thought'. 3 Everyday
empathy. 4 Restricted historical empathy – action understood by pupils 'by reference to
specific situations in which people found themselves: an appreciation of different values in the
past'. 5 Contextual historical empathy – where children attempt to fit what is to be understood
or explained into a wider picture '. . . the ability to speculate . . . an awareness that their own
standards are not the same as those of the past'.

secondary school may never reach this 'third' level. Nevertheless we should not restrict our expectations through the belief that primary children are unable to make a 'leap into the past' and sensitively respond to the predicaments of people long since dead.

In a dramatic reconstruction at the Tower of London, Aidan, aged ten,'met' Walter Raleigh, Bess his wife and King James I. Together with his class group he talked to the actors who themselves were reliving the past. On his return to school, steeped in the contextual elements of the lives of Walter, Bess and James, he wrote:

Three People

Three different people,
different personalities
Walter, inside a prison wall.
James a royal monarch.
Bess, Walter's wife, the centre of it all.

Walter was an explorer.
New lands he did seek
Gold, fruit and riches for all.

James hated Walter
Accused him of treason
Sentenced him to death
But kept him alive.

Bess helped Walter
Tried to set him free
Hoping that someday
He'd get out and survive.

James' son came to Walter
Walter educated him
When he became King,
Walter hoped he'd set him free.

But the boy, Henry, died
And Walter was left there
Thirteen years inside those hateful
walls.

For a share in the riches
One day King James set him free
So Walter set sail for Guiana
In his new ship 'Destiny'

Walter tried to find riches
James was cruel right to the end
Bess was ever ready to help
But the axe fell ...

In the first three lines Aidan identifies the main protagonists, showing feeling throughout his writing for Bess. He is aware of and sympathetic to the support she gave to Raleigh during his long imprisonment. He shares and identifies her hopes. He acknowledges and accepts the sadness and brutality of her ultimate failure. This example suggests that some ten-year-olds can be expected to go beyond everyday empathy and, whilst not achieving contextual historical empathy (ie level 5), are able to identify with some elements of situation in time past and accept that historical events cannot be evaluated simply in contemporary terms.

In these examples children attempted to enter into the past and to have a degree of sympathy with it. But to reflect in this way they had to acquire a whole range of facts with which to work and to be given the necessary skills which would enable them to interpret these facts with understanding.

This has implications for the teacher. It means that s/he needs to be aware of the spread of information which the children may want to tap. Skills which are central to any study – how to use reference books, how to collect and store information, how to interpret and present it – will have to be taught. Children are unlikely simply to acquire them. The way in which this is achieved (ie formally in a timetabled period or informally through actively doing) will be determined by the learning strategies adopted and encouraged within the school.

In my experience young children are able to identify with the past more readily if they are taken to places which have some historical significance, rather than if their exposure to history is limited to the page of a book. Imagination and a sensitivity to the human condition within a framework of time past is more easily fostered in young children if their senses can be sharpened. The priest's hole in a book can never be as threateningly claustrophobic as it was *in reality* for Ralph at Oxburgh Hall.

These basic skills provide the starting point. To them will need to be added one other element critical to any understanding of history. To empathise we need to be able to lose our 'twentieth-century-ness', the prejudices and expectations of our own time and somehow take on the attitudes and understanding of a past age; to see, for example, the world of a Roman legionary or an Edwardian lady's maid through *their* eyes, not our own.

This 'coming to know' through an amalgam of human feelings, historical evidence (considered below), an understanding of the backdrop to an historical epoch and the ability to shed contemporary prejudice – all of which are shaped and extended through the mastery of simple research techniques – makes considerable demands upon the young child. It is for this reason that in the early primary years we can foster only some of these elements. Talking through the story of 'Cinderella' with six-year-olds can evoke a feeling for her, but this should not be confused with historical empathy. Nevertheless confirmation *by the teacher* that human feelings for other people are worthy of comment will make children aware that this is a valid way of thinking. As they move towards the middle years of schooling and become capable of developing additional concepts and skills they will be more able to make a leap into the past and to personally respond to and identify with the period which is being 'relived'.

In this respect historical studies which invite children to have sensitivity for people living in time past may also be extended to topics which have a cross-cultural dimension. How do you think the Bristol slave trader viewed his cargo of African slaves? How might he have defended this trade? What do you think the slaves thought of these attitudes? Why are contemporary views likely to be so different from those which the trader probably held? Expansion of Empire might be a theme tackled by a primary school class. Some understanding of the impact of colonialism is more likely to be achieved if the children undertaking the study are helped to view European expansion from more than a single ethnocentric viewpoint.

One further rider applies. Younger children seem to find it easier to relate to an immediate past than to a distant one. For example, many teachers of five- and six-year-olds introduce the idea of the past by looking at the children's past – which, against the spread of historical time, is a very short period indeed. Often this look at the past is accomplished through family photographs, toys and baby clothes. The woollen booties worn by a five-year-old when he/she was a few days old are already historical artefacts. Moreover they are artefacts with which the child can identify. Compare them with the leather sandals for a medieval merchant. They fulfil a similar function but, having no personal relevance, they have little meaning for the child.

Simple observations of this kind cannot be presented as firm academic evidence. Yet we should not dismiss such observations out of hand. The effective teaching of young children is often accomplished through a process of decoding, ie the teacher helps the child towards understanding by taking an element within the child's personal world and unravelling it. Just as the abstractions of number can be clarified through examples drawn from everyday experience, so can reflections on personal time past lead the young child towards an entry into the study of history.

It is for this reason that many Year 3 and Year 4 classes approach history through the lives of the children and of their parents and grandparents. The timeline which invariably accompanies this study touches upon people whom they know and events about which they have probably learned through informal conversations, often overheard, between the adults in their lives. The changes in the short span of time which such a study encompasses are unlikely to be profound: contemporary prejudice is less likely to cloud understanding. Empathy does not *have* to span centuries.

Strategies – Empathy

1 Immerse children in an historical topic and ensure that a wide range of material (written, photographic, diagramatic) is available for them to use. The immersion might include visits to a museum, a film or a TV/video presentation. Towards the end of the topic encourage 'imagining'. The following was written by Jonathan, aged 10, to complete a study on 'Bartholomew Fair'.

Imagining . . .

I am a young lady. I am 28 years old and my name is Mary Elizabeth Hopkins. I work in Bartholomew Fair as a freak. I was born with the right size body and head, but out where my legs are supposed to be I have matchstick ankles and feet the size of a tiny box. When I was small, children would laugh at me because I looked like a monkey with my arms dragging along the ground. I had an unhappy childhood until I was 18, and then I was offered a job at Bartholomew Fair. They promised me money to appear as a freak. So I decided to show my terrible feet to the crowds, and as I'm different to other people, I

**would make the best of it. People started to admire me
instead of to laugh and snarl at me.**

2　Give children the opportunity to respond imaginatively to
the past by helping them to develop a sensitivity to place. This
necessitates giving children a contextual frame of reference upon
which to base their response. The example which follows was
written by Elspeth, a nine-year-old, as she stood on a disused
station platform.

The Station

A building stands deserted,
Weeds growing round it,
Long forgotten it stands,
In place of rails are weeds.
Here,
Where I'm standing,
Waiting for a train.
Ladies in long dresses
Men with bowler hats
Girls & boys playing along the platform
Would have heard a train . . .
But now the station stands deserted
Through all weathers it stands.
Forgotten.

3　Give children the opportunity to take part in re-enactments,
both within the school setting and on visits (see Chapter 4). This
will involve wearing historical costume and prompt questioning
eg 'How easy is it to sit and walk in a farthingale?' 'How do you
need to move your legs to avoid tripping over a dress sword?'
'How did people clean a greasy pot in the 17th century without
a plentiful supply of hot water and detergents?'

Encourage children to listen to, learn and play period music.

A re-enactment of a Victorian Christmas in a Lord of the Man-
or's house near Bodmin drew the following response from a
ten-year-old boy:

**I wouldn't have minded living in Victorian times, but I
wouldn't have wanted to be poor.**

4 Take children to museums which present an holistic view of a particular period of the past eg Yorvik Viking Museum, York or the Museum of the North East at Beamish, County Durham. Encourage children when on holiday to collect material (pictures, postcards, books etc) and make a classroom exhibition of the visit.

5 Visit an open museum where a traditional farmhouse or cottage is on view. Encourage children to focus on particular aspects, eg

- Heating and lighting in time past and today
- Kitchens. What does the modern kitchen tell us about developments in modern technology?

These investigations can form the background for a discussion on

- What do these elements tell us about the role of women *outside the house and home* – today and in the period of the past which is being investigated?

6 Encourage children to write to people in the past eg to protest to the Lord that the common has been enclosed for sheep grazing or that the village is to be demolished to make space for parkland around his new country house; to say that his support for the building of a school in the village is much appreciated.

Evidence

History, according to GR Elton, 'deals with the activities of men'.[13] Enquiry into these activities stems from examination of the evidence left behind by people who once lived. Evidence (buildings, artefacts or documents) gives the historian the base on which to build and enables him or her to move from the present into the past. Evidence uncorroborated by other sources is suspect. It might, like Piltdown man, *seem* to throw light on the past. It might also simply serve to confuse and obscure.

How can young children begin to move towards an understanding of 'what it is like to be an historian'? The generations of children who were brought up on textbooks which presented history as an unfolding story were rarely expected to question whether Richard III really murdered the princes in the Tower, or whether the contemporary evidence for attributing their deaths to him was anything more than circumstantial. In any event, should we make demands upon children which involve an understanding of political opportunism or of doctoring material in order to achieve a particular end? Can children relate to the vagaries of adult behaviour, essential if they are to be able to weigh the evidence which is presented?

In my experience, children are able, from about eight years old, to present their own views of adult behaviour. A group of ten- and 11-year-olds visited the Tower and subsequently the National Portrait Gallery. They then talked at length with their teacher about the Wars of the Roses and of the changing fortunes of the factions as they struggled to maintain power. One ten-year-old observed, 'Henry VII might have had the princes killed to make it easier for him to stay King'. This comment was followed by an equally pertinent, but much more childlike one 'anyway he wouldn't have said if he had. We all want to appear nice'. Undoubtedly children *do* have a capacity for insight and although this may be limited it can be developed through challenging classroom experiences. Figures 2.7–2.9 show an extended piece of classroom research.

Context and evidence

Questioning of the past is not limited to the weighing of motives. Children must be exposed to all manner of historical material. In suggesting that children must be encouraged to question, we find ourselves returning to a point already established ie that in order to develop methods of historical enquiry the learner must have some contextual framework within which to work.

A group of ten-year-olds are examining the holes in the porch door of Alton church in Hampshire. They are unlikely, without some knowledge of the Civil War, to arrive at a guess as to why the holes are there. They look around the church for supporting evidence of a battle which they have learned about from a selection of contemporary written evidence which they have studied at school. Their response, in consequence, is sensitive. Were the holes to fire through or to spy through? Could the door provide protection against a troop of well-trained Roundheads? How much of the entrance can one musket cover? Where else could defenders be safely placed?

This initial exploration gives young children a starting point, but little more. It serves only to prompt further questioning. Can we accept the evidence in and around the church? Does the evidence we

Figure 2.7 *A group of 11-year-olds were given some Victorian clothes. They were used for research and the children's findings were displayed.*

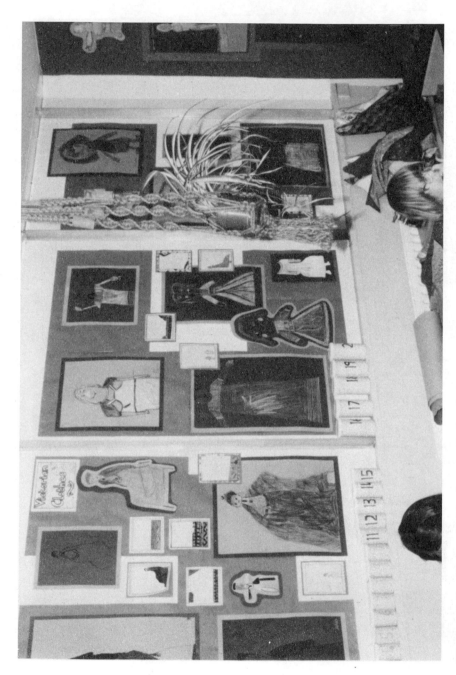

Figure 2.8 *Six-year-olds then used the clothes as primary source material.*

Figure 2.9 *The interest in the period led the older children to the construction of Victorian games.*

see confirm the contemporary accounts? Who wrote them? Did the Royalists who defended the church seek to create a legend about the bravery of their commander? Is there a Puritan viewpoint? Where else can we look for evidence? How is the engagement presented in Alton Museum? Does it reflect the facts we established? If not, how do they differ? Questions of detail but of significance also emerged from this study. If the defenders were able to repel the Roundheads for some hours they must have been well-trained marksmen. How quickly could one man fire, reload and fire a 17th Century musket? What were the women and children doing meanwhile?

Questions like those posed above are rooted in three distinct areas – the knowledge and understanding which each child has acquired before visiting the church, the experience of the site itself and finally, the coming together of these two elements. If the third state, understanding at a deeper level, can be achieved then the child has the foundation upon which to base further questions. These questions may be specific to the event or set the event within a broader historical context. It follows that the teacher's task is to bring children into situations where evidence is available and to help them to both question and be aware of the provisionality of their findings. This will help develop questioning skills which, provided they are used throughout the years of education which follow primary schooling, will become personal to each child.

A focus on evidence encourages children to see the historian as a 'detective in time' for 'everything a man says, or writes, everything he makes, everything he touches can and ought to teach us about him.' This has a natural appeal to children. The medieval arrowhead is not itself history. But using it as a starting point gives the enquirer a tiny part of a picture – a picture which he or she can start to fill in.

The enquiry which follows the handling of the arrowhead should be designed to deepen the child's level of understanding by extending the range of questions asked. What does this arrowhead tell us about medieval warfare, the craftsmen who fashioned it, the soldier who fired it? Then, broadening the discussion, we could ask how we know that this *is* a medieval arrowhead. This type of questioning is even more rewarding when applied to the recorded actions of people in history and to the written documents which they have left to explain their actions. Was it brave or foolhardy of Nelson to place a telescope to his blinded eye and so to ignore the signal to withdraw? Had Eisenhower failed at the battle of Normandy or had the Charge of the Light Brigade been a great success would we view these two historical events from a different perspective? The need to develop, through questioning, an informed scepticism of events present as well as past has never been greater. Reflections of this kind apply as keenly to the sinking of the *Belgrano* in 1982 as to that of the *Titanic* in 1912, the changing face of the USSR in the 1980s or the devastation of the Basra road in 1991.

Trying to discover the truth, discovering what 'probably happened' should be a central ingredient of the teaching of history. The element of uncertainty, presenting a number of sides of a question and weighing evidence is too often omitted from school history books and from the practical activities which the books support. A mass of received facts and the recapitulation of well-used stories (in which kings and queens remain labelled in folk tradition as 'good', 'weak', 'wise' or 'unready') gives children a smattering of pseudo-history and nothing of the real nature of its discipline.

The problem of working with evidence is that young children initially have a very uninformed framework within which to relate it. Yet the object itself often prompts research and results in a framework being constructed. The flexibility and improvisation that this assumption presupposes should be a characteristic of every primary classroom. Improvisation is one of the skills of the historian. It is also an essential ingredient of good classroom practice (see Chapter 5).

Strategies for teaching evidence

1 Provide children with a poster from a past period of history (eg World War I or World War II). What can be gleaned from it?

2 Provide a group of children with a handbag which has been 'found'. In it there are a variety of objects eg a single adult railway ticket, three low denomination foreign banknotes, a car key on a fob, an empty medicine box bearing the name Mary O'Malley, a bus timetable with a destination marked in red ink, a scrap of paper bearing a Dublin telephone number, a letter written to 'Mum' and signed 'love John', a photograph of two children with 'To Nan' on the back and a spectacle case. *What can be deduced from the contents about the owner of the bag? What things can we be certain about? How much is inspired guesswork?*

(The same kind of activity can be based upon a wallet, a purse or a collection of old clothes with odd articles in the pockets.)

3   Use a collection of old photographs or engravings of a local landmark (eg town square, High Street) to provide a starting point for a study of evidence for continuity and change. *Which buildings remain? Which have disappeared? Can we be sure that the photographs are accurately dated? Are the changes noted also shown on maps published over the period being studied?*

4   Collect a range of advertisements and items of sales literature. *What do they tell us about life today? Are advertisements always truthful? Might they contain bias?*
Provide children with advertisements from the recent past (1900 onwards) – local museums will usually be able to provide photocopies. *What do they tell us about life during the period in which they were published?*

5   On a visit to a museum, monastic ruin, castle or similar site encourage children to focus upon one element of a larger whole. For example, instead of drawing a whole suit of armour the focus could be upon the decoration on the breast plate or upon the technology involved in the hinge on the helmet or the wheeled spur; instead of suggesting that each child draw the entire castle the focus for one child might be window shapes, for another patterns in wood and stone, for a third heraldic crests. This narrowing of focus supports children who cannot draw a complete knight or cope with an architectural sketch. (It also helps develop the skill of detailed observation.) The individual drawings should be supported by a written account to set them within a broader context. *What does one element of a larger artefact tell us about the historic past?*

6   Make a classroom museum of things which might be useful evidence of how we live today. The museum table could feature such things as an advertisement for a beauty product, a phonecard, an empty coke bottle, a newspaper, the wrapping from a packet of frozen food, a microwave dish, a bus or rail ticket, a commemorative stamp, an SF toy, a football supporter's scarf, the photograph of a pop group, a copy of *TV Times*, a strip of 'velcro', a ball-point pen, a solar-powered calculator, a piece of wallpaper, a recycled paper bag, a plastic carrier, a tube of toothpaste with a 'flip' lid . . .

7   Announce that the school is going to be demolished. Invite

the children to make accurate drawings and/or photographs of three things they would wish to record to show how schools were used in the 1990s. What notes would be needed to accompany the drawings?

8 Eyewitness reports. These may take many forms and include direct reports from official enquiries; diaries (eg Pepys' Diaries); newspapers which record a particular event (eg *The Times* reporting the victory at Trafalgar) and letters (eg the Paston letters). It is possible to supplement written accounts of more recent events with sound recordings (eg the description of the Hindenberg disaster on 6 May 1937). Figure 2.10 shows a pupil's 'eyewitness account' from 1939, which can be used as a source of historical evidence.

A TRIBUTE TO A BERMONDSEY MOTHER

My Mother is a nice lady. She is 5 ft tall and 3 ft wide. She has a rough red face and pointed nose, which gets shiny when it is not powdered. She has no force teeth, but her front teeth are broken. She is forty, which in these days is not considered old. She takes size 6 shoes and wears a green coat. She was brought up rough and ready, and believes in us being brought up like it. She is married. She married my father at St. James when she was 18. She has 8 more children besides me, and she says she would not be without one of us. We have 2 bedrooms and one kitchen.

Every morning she goes office cleaning at 5, stepping soft so as not to wake us. She meets her mates at the tram. She leaves our lunch packets and milk pennies on the dresser. Dad gets our breakfast before he goes to look for work. She gets home before we start for school, and sees we are tidy. Then she puts on her pinliesfore and starts housework. She sweeps the rooms, makes the beds, does the shopping, peels the potatoes, cooks twelve dinners, one for Gran, who lives ten doors away. She is a good cook and can cook anything possible. Dinner is always ready when we get back. After she has washed up, there is a lot to do. She has regular days for everything. Mondays and Thursdays she scrubs the rooms. Tuesday is washing day. This is the only day she grumbles. Wednesday and Friday she mends our clothes, which are always getting tore. Saturdays she goes to the Blue to get our stores. She takes my sister to learn her the trade of bargoning the butcher. At 4, she gets tea. If it is rore, she cooks it. At 5 she has to go office cleaning again. And gets home at 9 and puts us to bed. She brings us cocoa in bed. She keeps on the go all day and never sits down. She looks after the sick baby upstairs while its mother is at work. She says its lucky for us there's no eight hour day for mothers. She says its lucky for us work is her hobby.

She gets mad if we are untidy. She says the sign of her home is Spick and span. If we throw caps on the dresser, on the floor they go. Sometimes I make her wild when I'm a terrer, and she gives me a good highden. She uses her hand, but it hurts. This is seldom though. When dad tries to hit us she stops him and he gets Jord. Once I stop out late. Did I get it. Never no more do I stop out late.

She has to go carefy with her money now dad is out of work. Sometimes she worries awful over the rent. She has lots of worries, but she keeps them to herself. She doesn't care much about herself, if we are alright. She always has a smile round the corners of her mouth, and tells us funny things to make us laugh. She likes us to read comics. She likes to hear sporty things over the wireless, like Larry Gains v Len Harvey, but if I try to get a long distance and it starts isolating, there is trobel. Her favourite star is Gracie Fields, and her favourite team is the Arsenal. She doesn't drink much except at holidays. She is very friendly with the neighbours. Al her life she says she has never had a quarrel with a neighbour. If I take one of my mates in, she gives him a cup of tea and a cake. Every day she throws crums to the sparrows. The only thing wrong with her is she wont let me have a bike.

She learns me manners. She tells me not to sorce people older than myself. She is decended from a very old Bermondsey family. She has always lived in Bermondsey and says she would never like to live anywhere else. When she dies, I shall miss her terribly.

Figure 2.10 *The child as eye-witness. This piece was written by an 11-year-old child. It is included in full (including errors) as an example which can be used in class discussion and as a reminder that evidence of the past is to be found in the most unlikely places – in this case a school essay written in 1939.*

Cause and effect

Enquiries of the kinds outlined in the various 'strategies' included in this chapter will help children towards some understanding of cause and a realisation that most events have a multiplicity of causes. 'Genuine historical explanations are necessarily tentative, demand qualifications and must admit to exceptions'.[14] Historians attempt to unravel the link between an event and the numerous and varied elements which may have occasioned it.

All-too-often textbooks present young readers with too simplistic a reason behind an event (see book selection, pp 133–139). It is much more valuable for children to be helped to realise that events which we regard as significant are often shaped over quite long periods of time. For example, although Wilbur Wright's heavier than air machine flew at a particular time (17 Dec 1903) and at a particular place (Kitty Hawk, North Carolina) the event was really a culmination of a long series of technological and scientific discoveries (events in themselves) which had been made over many centuries.

Strategies – Cause and effect

1   Encourage children to analyse a quarrel. The quarrel (and perhaps the fisticuffs) were the event. *How many causes contributed to the altercation? Did these causes have their roots in different periods of time past?*

2   Record a simple game in pictures, words or by recording each number thrown on the dice – snakes and ladders, draughts or, for more sophisticated children, chess. *What series of happenings contributed to victory/defeat? For example, how, in chess, did the King come to be exposed? Had one specific move not been made, might the result (checkmate) have been different?*

At first sight it might seem that questions of the type suggested in the strategy activities outlined here presuppose that children have a full contextual framework against which to respond – and, of course, this is unlikely to be the case. In discussing human actions in the past and in encouraging the presentation of possible alternatives we help children to understand that people respond to situations in a variety of ways and that their responses will be determined by a wide range of attitudes, feelings and beliefs.

However, it is not *only* these elements which condition response. Individual men and women cannot be detached themselves from the political, economic and social forces of their age. These, too, have shaped (and continue to shape) their daily lives. To present Charles I, for example, as one who died for his belief in the divine nature of Kingship is but a half truth. The problems which beset him could equally well be ascribed to the inflationary effects of gold from the New World as to religious idealism or Stuart stubbornness.

The raising of such issues is central to the teaching of history. There will be some children from whom such discussions will provoke little response. Conceptually they may not be ready to face such issues. For many ten and 11-year-olds, such ideas *do* matter. Young children may not have the ability to distance themselves from an event or to be impartial and yet this of itself can be of value. Bombs are dropped on Tripoli by American bombers based in England in peacetime. Is it moral to kill in order to stop killing?

In passing it is worth nothing that contemporary issues (like a bomb outrage, the demolition of the Berlin Wall, the freeing of a South African activist) are taken by TV into children's homes. 'History-present' provides teachers with a wide range of discussion topics. The majority of the children will have gleaned some information from the media and the understanding so gained can be explored through class discussion. When children have developed the confidence to discuss 'history-present', sustained discussion about 'history-past' becomes more manageable – particularly if, when current issues are examined, some thought is given to the ways in which information is presented and the possibility of prejudice explored.

Thus we could say that teaching children historical concepts helps them understand the values which are central to our society. As we have seen above, it may also equip them to question contemporary issues and free themselves of prejudice. It would be foolish to believe, however, that this admirable state of affairs is dependent solely on the quality of history teaching in schools. A variety of academic inputs contribute to children's development of a range of life skills: history is but one element, albeit an important one.

Children also need words in order to be able to share their thoughts with others. Like all academic disciplines, history has its own specialist terms and phrases. Children should be encouraged to express historical ideas in their own way. 'Renaissance' 'power' 'epoch' 'reformation' 'justice' have specific and clear meanings. The seven-year-old who describes a situation as 'sort of unfair' is grappling with the concept of justice at her level, just as is the nine-year-old who described 'power' as 'control over what other people want'. Children in the middle years of schooling are well able to appreciate the meaning of historical terms, so long as they are dressed in an image which can be grasped. The medium, as it were, shapes the message. The idea of poverty, for example, is much more directly grasped by reading a description from Dickens or Mayhew or by watching a newsreel clip of women and children from the Horn of Africa desperate for food than through a clinical dictionary definition.

The spiral curriculum

The viewpoints advanced above support my belief that at an early stage of school life (and here the general level of individual maturity and the ability to communicate meaningfully is more significant than calendar age) children should be introduced to the 'idea' underlying historical method. This means that children will be learning concepts and a particular way of entering into the 'subject' that they are considering. Further, this approach will be repeated in a deeper, more profound way as they move through school. It has been described by Bruner as a spiral curriculum. As the spiral develops it should:

> Revisit basic ideas, repeatedly building upon them until the student has grasped the full formal apparatus that goes with them.[15]

In the model advanced by Bruner the elements of the discipline are more significant than the content. What is learned is a number of linked frames of reference, the significance and relevance of each frame becoming ever more clear as contextual knowledge is acquired. 'The child's way of viewing things'[16] becomes the bridge which carries process into content. For if the *nature* of intellectual activity for all humans is everywhere the same, then children will think as adults think ... 'the difference is in degree, not in kind'[17]. This assumes, of course, that the concepts can be clearly and honestly identified!

So the task of the teacher in presenting history begins not with the presentation of dead facts, neither should he or she be trapped into introducing the processes used by historians against a predeter-mined, age-based programme. The spiral should take children from the level of understanding they have achieved through a graded sequence of representations. In doing so they move from the simple and the concrete to the complex and the abstract, acquiring the underlying principles that give structure to the subject.

Presented in this way, the teaching of history to young children is centred upon process, the development of attitudes in the way the children evaluate information they are given or discover about the past and the acquisition of skills at a level appropriate to the individual abilities of each child. Through this approach children will learn how to organise the present information in an historical way, how to 'find out' how to evaluate the facts they discover and how to communicate their findings. Their vocabulary will expand as they use the particular and specific words they need to explain their findings.

References

1   Dearden R F, Hint P H, Peters P H *Education and the development of reason* RKP, London, 1972, p 251.
2   Fines, John *History Today* Vol. 39, June 1989, p 9.
3   Bloch, Marc *The Historian's Craft* Manchester University Press, 1984 edition p. 26.
4   West, John *Teaching History No. 32* Feb 1982 pp 33–35 and *Trends in Education* Spring Issue, 1978.
5   Blyth, Joan *Teaching History, No. 21* June 1978 pp 16–18.
6   Hexter, J H *On Historians* Collins, London 1979, p 94.
7   DES *History in the Primary and Secondary years – an HMI view* HMSO, London 1985, p 4.
8   Jahoda, Gustav 'Children's concepts of time and history' *Educational Review* Vol. 15, No. 2, University of Birmingham 1963, p 94.
9   DES *History in the Primary and Secondary Years* op cit p 59, op cit p 3.
10 Unstead R J *Teaching History in the Junior School* A & C Black, London, 1959, p 4.
11 Bloch, Marc *op cit* p 44.
12 Lee P J 'History Teaching and the "Philosophy of History" ' in *Philosophy of History* Vol XXII, No 4, Beiheft.
13 Dickinson, AK et al *Learning History* Heinemann, London, 1984 p 106.
14 Bloch, Marc *op cit* p 66.
15 Bruner, J S *The Process of Education* Knopt Vintage Books/ New York and Harvard University Press 1960, p 13.
16 *ibid* p 33.
17 *ibid* p 33.

3 School-centred approaches

Beware of cultural amnesia, the source of barbarism . . .
Yves Pelicier, UNESCO Conference, Paris, 1989

In the final Report of the National Curriculum History Working Group the nature of historical knowledge is presented as follows:

- *Knowledge as information*: the basic facts, for example, events, places, dates, names.
- *Knowledge as understanding*: the facts studied in relation to other facts and evidence about them and placed in an explanatory framework which enables their significance to be perceived.
- *Knowledge as content*: the subject matter of study, for example, a period or a theme.

If the nature of historical knowledge is to be grasped (the Report continues) the relationship between these elements needs to be grasped. 'In the study of history the essential objective must be the acquisition of knowledge as understanding . . . knowledge as understanding cannot be achieved without a knowledge of historical information.' The task of the teacher (if we follow Bruner's model) is therefore to use process as a means of unlocking information which may then be examined in such a way as to further historical understanding and deepen the young learner's appreciation of what it is to be an historian, ie a difference in degree but not in kind.

The following approaches provide a ready means for achieving these ends.

History through family studies

'I can remember being sent to prison. You see, I was a suffragette. I wanted women to be able to vote. But they let me out when the war started. They needed us nurses to go to the front and look after injured soldiers.'

These are the words of a 90-year-old in conversation with a group of junior school children in 1976. (She subsequently celebrated her 100th birthday on a visit to the school.)

For young children an appropriate place to begin the study of history is in the here and now, through individual studies within the family unit and through people who live in the area around their home and school. Approaching a study of history through the present opens a way through which each child is able to relate the past to their own *personal position* in time. Once this point is clearly fixed, a journey through or into the past is more easily understood.

Family studies are therefore a way of looking at a microcosm of time. Indeed, some educationalists even go so far as to suggest that those children who have an extended family and who are in regular contact with their grandparents are likely to develop a more soundly rooted sense of time than are those whose contact with older people is somewhat limited. This suggests that if all children are to be given the opportunity to develop a sense of 'generational time' schools should facilitate the coming together of the young and the old. Put more simply, family studies in all their different forms establish each individual as being part of history. Being human we all have a past.

The use of an immediate and personal past also provides some idea of the importance of the roots which each individual has in a local, national and international community. At the same time it indicates something of the continuity of the human race.

The implications of this need for 'roots' are daunting. The study of the actions of people in the past is enormous in its scope and, for most of us, quite impossible to grasp fully. If children are to begin to understand the magnitude of the study, then the past needs to be graspable, comprehensible. This suggests that we should try to avoid a history curriculum which sets out to progress from time long past to time present. All too often the journey consumes the whole of the primary years so that the contemporary scene is rarely examined in depth. One has only to look through publishers' booklists to discover how pervasive this approach is. Teachers of children in Year 3 are offered information on cavemen and dinosaurs in large print, short sentences and many pictures. For older year groups, the typeface progressively shrinks, the sentences grow longer, the pictures diminish in impact and quantity.

This is not to argue that history must be taught backwards. To do so for any extended period would be to confuse rather than clarify the idea that history comments upon the subtle metamorphosis which unites times past with times present. Rather it is to suggest that one way into history is to use the here and now to give some meaning to a study of the past.

Children undertaking such work begin with the present, asking such questions as 'Who am I?' 'Who are my parents?'. These initial questions are not essentially historical. 'Who am I?' may invite reflection on one's personality or on the significance of the individual when set against the cosmos. Nevertheless, the direction which the children follow is historical. The second set of questions: 'Who was my mother's mother? Where was she born?' requires each child to look to the past for evidence. Having found an answer, the child goes on to question its validity. 'How can I be certain that *this* Ann Smith is the person I am seeking?' 'Does this new fact confirm my other findings or conflict with them?' 'How can I take my new extended findings further?' 'How does it relate to material that I already have?'

When using pupils' own histories as a means of exploring the past and developing some understanding of basic methodology, the material offered by each child must be received with thought and sensitivity. A child whose father has recently left home, or one whose grandmother has just died, can be excused for showing little enthusiasm for family studies.

For the accomplished teacher this topic will provide all manner of cross-curricular links: family portraits painted and drawn; collage pictures of episodes in family life; mathematics based upon personal height and weight, span and foot measures; the surface area of feet and hands followed by group and class graphs and mappings of the statistics obtained; geographical studies exploring family 'roots', favourite foods and where they are harvested; multicultural issues addressed through a study of celebrations, festivals, dietary rules, mother tongue, beliefs and customs. The initial starting point may be historical, but since many of the activities described above require the children to record in words (handwritten or word-processed) the possibilities are almost limitless.

Through such personal enquiries into the past children realise that historical enquiry can lead to unexpected discoveries. Anika, an 11-year-old, had written a book about her family. It was called 'Me' and was illustrated with photocopies of source material, family photographs, some newspaper cuttings and several family trees. Glancing through the pages I found a section entitled 'Uncle Eric'. I learned that Eric had spent many years in prison. 'Not that I mind,' observed Anika, 'about Uncle Eric, I mean. Everybody has something like that somewhere hidden away.' This remark hinted at Anika's maturity but it also suggested to me that she had been fortunate in working with a sensitive and thoughtful teacher. Entry into a family's past can cause pain and tension. Parental involvement is therefore to be encouraged and alerted before such a study is undertaken.

But let us for a moment return to the example provided by Anika's Uncle Eric. Before she began her enquiry Anika did not know that her uncle had spent time in prison. Indeed until she began her study she was unaware that her mother ever had a brother. Perhaps, without being aware of it, she had been led, incidentally, to realise that the study of history is about people who are capable of pursuing conscious ends. In a situation where outcomes cannot be certain both teacher and child become learners, enquirers, seekers after information.

The great value of these studies, however, is that the past is shown as *real*. The members of Anika's family were born, lived, married, worked, moved from one place to another, had children, died – just as people do today. They are more than just fictional characters (who are mere puppets in the hands of a gifted writer). Each of the people Anika discovered had responded to the everyday pressures and circumstances of the times in which they lived.

For the young child the most appropriate route into history is in discovering that *each human being* has a history. By personalising history we help free the subject of heavy academic overtones and yet provide rich material for analysis. The following case study looks at family history in practice.

Case study – Family history

A class of seven-year-olds were involved in a project called 'Who am I?'. It had been introduced through a series of informal talk sessions. The teacher asked questions designed to prompt reflection:

- *Can you remember something which happened to you when you were very small?*
- *Can you remember your first day at school? What can you tell me about it?*

- *Have you any photographs at home which show what you looked like when you were small?*

This last question encouraged a number of children to bring photographs of themselves 'when they were young'. The teacher added a photograph of herself as a baby to the resulting wall display, emphasising as she did so that everybody has a past and that in Western societies that past is often captured in pictures. The display was now a central feature of the classroom. What could be added to it? Very quickly it was extended to include a varied collection of baby clothes and toys. 'These bootees were my big brother's too. So they are older than me and as old as him.'

The photographs and artefacts were then used to lead children towards the idea of evidence. 'How can we be *sure* this is a picture of John?' evinced an unexpected response from Peter. 'This is me' (pointing to a photograph of a toddler) 'This is my Mum. So you could ask my Mum whether this is me and her.'

The idea of 'asking Mum' for corroboration was seized upon by several of the class. It allowed the teacher to move the discussion into oral history: 'If we asked older people about the past, what might they be able to tell us?' A list was compiled from the children's response to this question. It was closely related to home life and included such things as clothes, shopping, food, getting to school and holidays.

At this point the teacher decided to use the questions to create a structure which would allow the children to do some research of their own. A form was prepared for children to take home. It took the form of a letter (See Figure 3.1) and included a suggestion that the recipients might even like to arrange to visit the class and share their early memories with small groups of children.

The response was most rewarding. The oldest person to respond to the request was over 90 years old, the youngest in his mid-40s. Some of the visitors brought books and artefacts which related to their own childhood. A few of these were loaned to the class for incorporation in the display – a flat iron, some postcards, a war medal, a washing board. These complemented items supplied by the children's parents, the family

Dear *

Our class is trying to find out what it was like when you
were seven years old.
We are interested in:

<u>Going to school</u>

What was school like when you were seven?

How many children were in your class?

What things did you learn?

What sort of games did you play at playtime?

Did you walk to school or go by car, train or bus?

<u>Clothes</u>

What sort of clothes did you wear?

Were the clothes of grown-ups different from the clothes
grown-ups wear today?

<u>Washing and cleaning</u>

How did your mother do the washing?

How did your mother clean the house?

Did your dad help?

<u>Food</u>

Where did your mother go to buy food?

What sort of things did she cook?

What sort of lighting did you have?

Is there anything else you could tell me?

If you would like to come to school to talk to us about
some of these things Mrs Brown, my teacher, would be
pleased to meet you.

Thank you for helping

   *   (signed by child)

* The letter was personalised by each child using a vdu and printer. Thus the letters were
addressed variously to Grandpa, Pop, Nan, Granny, Mrs Jones, Aunty Meg – and ended with
such expressions as 'love', 'See you Thursday', 'Hope you are well'.

Figure 3.1

photographs displayed often spanning three or four generations. Whenever appropriate the children's attention was drawn to the classroom timeline on which were marked the more significant elements of the study.

Although much of the material presented to the children was oral, some was recorded on tape. The children recorded simple accounts. 'Mrs Griffiths came to school today. She told us she was a nurse. She was also a suffragette. She was taken to the police station for wanting women to vote.'

The activity was used by the teacher to support other curriculum areas. Its main focus, however, was upon how best to examine and classify the information which had been gathered. The idea of oral evidence was discussed, *physical* evidence (like the flat iron) was used for handling exercises (see page 42) and *pictorial* evidence (the photographs) and *documentary* evidence (a ration book) were related to the events which had been described by visitors and parents.

One unexpected diversion was an exploration of where people lived 30 or 40 years ago. It began with the comment: 'Old people never seem to move!' This was not a reflection on current mobility but an observation that the 'oldest' people seemed to have lived near the school for most of their lives. Few of the parent group had been 'local babies'. Why should there be this difference?

Another particularly valuable aspect of the project was the way in which children questioned the oral presentations. 'How could Mrs Griffiths remember so good?' The teacher's response was in the form of another question. 'Can we always believe what people tell us? Should Simon believe what his Gran told him last Saturday? If Simon tells us what his Gran said, how do we know that Simon is saying exactly what she said?'

This study took longer than half a term to complete. The findings and displays were then transferred to the school library for other children in the school to see and to share. For this second level presentation, books illustrating particular elements thrown up by the study were built into the display (eg books on trams; World War II, home front; the suffragettes).

Following a lead from present into past can help children realise that the historian does not begin with an idea (eg 'King John was bad') and seek evidence to prove it. Rather s/he follows strands of evidence which, when looked at together, indicate probability: 'a condition of likelihood'. In passing it is worth noting that the questions which young children ask when beginning an enquiry (be it about the life of the honey bee or the stone effigy of a medieval knight) can rarely be set within a particular academic discipline. The task of the teacher is to take the question and, through discussion, lead the questioner towards the methods that will help him or her uncover the answer; in addition, the teacher needs to encourage the learner to appreciate that certain methods are more appropriate to one academic discipline than to another.

Enquiries of this type involve drawing upon memories and recollections of older people in the community, again helping to develop in young children the skills of questioning against a backdrop of time past. 'The collected memory of a community,' to quote Bernard Lewis, 'may not always be accurate, it may contain bias or untruth.'[1] Teachers need to be aware of this, but alert, too, to the excellent opportunity this provides to discuss the value and place of unsupported oral evidence.

There is one further reservation. It may indeed be true that 'when an old person dies it is as if a whole library was going up in flames' (African proverb). Nevertheless we must beware of so concentrating upon the rooting of history within the local community that we encourage enthnocentrism and fail to develop an understanding of other civilisations and other points of view.

Family studies, while confirming one's own personal links with the past, may, if followed too exclusively, tend to obscure from children the fact that we live in a world in which many contrasting cultures co-exist. Just as children need to appreciate the culture which has provided the structure and pattern of their own family life; they also need to be helped to appreciate the cultural heritage of the nation state in which they live and of the world community. The child of immigrant parents working in Birmingham must be given opportunities throughout his or her school life to experience both the cultural and historical past of the family and those of the state in which the family is now living. This means that an awareness of cultural pluralism should be addressed throughout the curriculum so that cultures and histories other than that of the 'parent nation' are shown to be of value and significance.

One way of realising this would be to actively seek to invite older people from communities outside the immediate area of school to share some of their life experience with the class. A leader of a nearby Jewish community might be invited to tell of his early childhood experiences as a refugee in post-war Europe, a child who came to England by boat with her parents from Jamaica in the early 1950s could comment on the differences she recognises between childhood now and childhood then. One of my most moving memories as a teacher illustrates this. A Grandfather (a Polish Jew) gave of his time over a period of several weeks to work in a class of five- to eight-year-olds. He explained to them, in small groups, his craft as a carpenter, 'how my hands came to know tools, my fingers to read wood'. His work in school coincided with a period of intense personal grief (the death of his wife, with whom as a child he escaped from Poland at the onset of the holocaust). Recalling and sharing his past with the young (including his grandson), eased his grief and helped him to begin living once more.

Family history (which in a school in which I worked was successfully used with five, six and seven-year-olds) leads naturally into a study of the local community itself. 'When I was young,' a grandmother talking to a group of eight-year-olds recalled, 'there was a brewery where the supermarket now stands. Outside it, on the pavement, was a gentleman's toilet. The toilet was bombed during the war. Now another one is being built on the same spot – but for women as well as men'. Examples of this kind help young children to grasp the fact that there is continuity between history and now. In focusing upon something as commonplace as a public convenience, the grandparent also illustrated quite accidentally that entry into an historical study can have the most inauspicious beginnings.

As Wingsley points out, the details which are often revealed in such encounters provide material for what could be described as 'micro history':

> The practice of sociologists and social anthropologists ... underline the strength of the strategic position of the family in studies of social change, class, the socialisation process and political and economic behaviour.'[2]

Strategies – Family studies

1 Family studies may begin with the simple questions:

- *Who am I?*
- *Who are my parents?*

These questions might be followed by others:

- *Where was I born?*
- *Where and when were my parents born?*
- *Where did my parents grow up?*
- *When and where did they meet?*
- *Have they always lived here?*
- *If not, where did they live before?*
- *Did they have brothers and sisters?*
- *Where are they now?*
- *Who were my mother's parents?*
- *Where did they live?*
- *Who were my father's parents?*
- *Where did they live?*
- *What work did my (two) grandfathers/grandmothers do?*
- *How much did they earn per week?*
- *What would this money buy?*

There are numerous questions which children can devise along these lines – questions about clothing, food, schooling, entertainment, housing, housework, travel ...

2 Encourage children to bring family photographs to school (see Figures 3.2–3.5). Most photographic shops provide a cheap copying service and if old photographs are to be used in a wall display it might be wise to use copies rather than originals. Figure 3.6 shows a classroom display of items brought in by five- to seven-year-olds.

3 Construct family trees. This activity has many links with mathematics and computer studies.

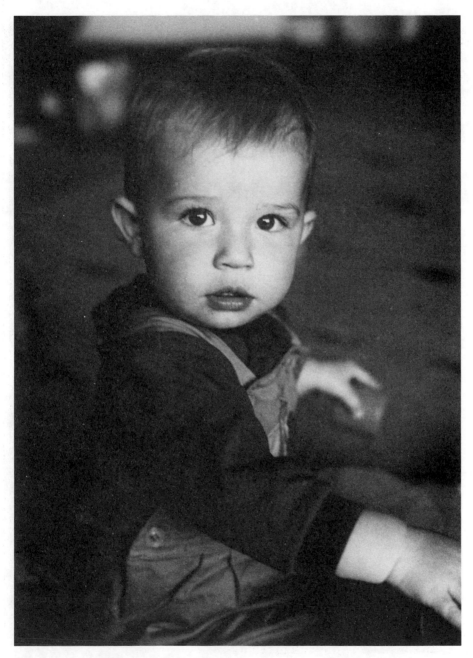

Figure 3.2 *This is me when I was a baby.*

Figure 3.3   *My mummy was a baby. She looked like this.*

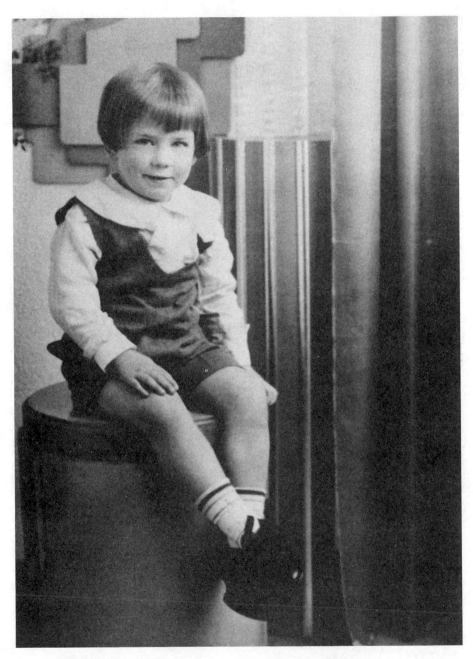

Figure 3.4 *This is my mummy's Daddy. I call him Grumps.*

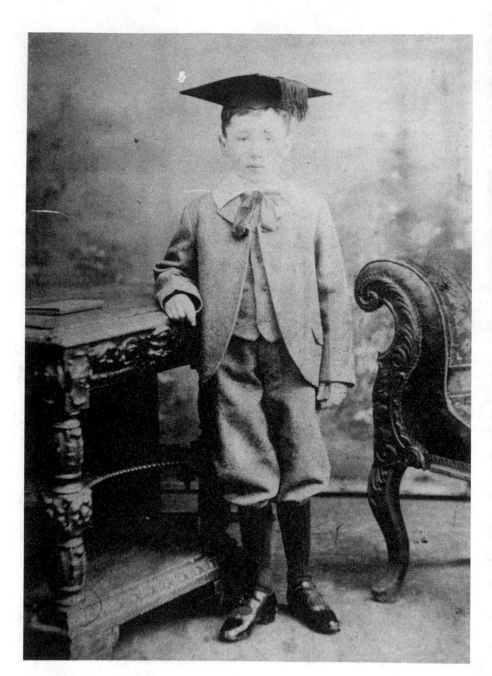

Figure 3.5   *This is my Grumps Daddy. He was a baby too.*

Figure 3.6   *Classroom display, five- to seven-year-olds.*

History through community studies

We shall not cease from exploration
And the end of all our exploring
Will be to arrive where we started
And know the place for the first time.
Through the unknown . . .
In that which was the beginning.

T S Eliot *Little Gidding* Stanza V

The local community is frequently used as a starting point for historical enquiry. This has many advantages. First, it indicates to children that history is all around them: that the Peabody Buildings in which they live reflect and comment upon 19th century values and attitudes as cogently as the workhouse that is now used as an NHS hospital, or Darlington Railway Station or the Palace of Westminster.

Second, local studies develop the idea of looking for evidence in a particular way, how the environment has been shaped through time, the materials that have been used and the techniques adopted. This 'looking in depth' invariably raises a number of other questions:

- Why was the site chosen?
- Who chose it?
- When?
- How did it develop?
- What materials have been used?
- Where did they come from?
- Where did we find additional information to confirm, amend or challenge these views?

Visual awareness is a skill which can be developed in the great majority of children. The idea of becoming a 'visual detective' has an almost universal appeal.[3] The discovery, for example, of a square of neatly-kept Stuart almshouses – dwarfed by derelict warehouses and scruffy workshops spilling out of railway arches – led one group of ten-year-olds to the county record office. The worry was historical, but human in its dimensions: how could anyone build a railway line so close to old people who needed 'peace and quiet'? Such a question parallels the 'Why should this be?' of the professional historian.

Local studies, sensitively planned and executed, allow teachers to develop material which is related to the pupils' everyday lives.

Through experiencing the past children come to appreciate something of the significance of the commonplace present. 'Knowing', at
this level, will include the excitement which comes from the
discovery that they and their family have a part in society past and
present, and their slowly developing ability to unravel the implications behind the things they see.

Jeffrey Toms of the Education Department of the Museum of
London describes this knowing and understanding of place as
'landscape history' and sees it as an unrivalled means of entering
the past.

Strategy – Asking questions about a building

Whatever the building (Roman fort, Norman church, Victorian
station, modern airport) certain questions can be asked about
it:

- *When was it built?*
- *Why was it built?*
- *Why was this site chosen?*
- *Who built it?*
- *What materials have been used in its construction:*
  for walls; roofing; floors; ceilings?
- *Is the building still used for its original function?*
- *Is there evidence of repair, rebuilding or extension?*
- *Is the building still being used? If not, when was it last*
  occupied? Why is it now vacant?
- *Can you find evidence of this building in engravings, drawings,*
  photographs?
- *Can you find evidence of this building on historical maps?*
- *Can you find out how much the building cost when it was*
  originally constructed?
- *Can you find out anything about the building methods used in*
  its construction (eg tools and equipment) and the size of the
  labour force which was required to build it?

To tap the local environment demands imaginative teaching.
Children will need to develop an understanding of context, the
framework within which the buildings were erected and their
function, as well as learning something about the various 'power'

groups which were behind their construction (church, central government, local government, entrepreneur, local or national landowner).

Training children's eyes to read a landscape, to observe and understand is not appropriate only for schools in cathedral cities or country villages which can boast a stately home or antique ruins. Every school has been built within a 'space' which can be interpreted. One ten-year-old, having followed a number of urban trails planned by the teacher as part of a four-year programme of environmental study, wrote:

> **You can tell roughly when a house was built by the style of the windows and doors, the material used for the roof, the style of brickwork. But if a house has all the evidence of a Victorian house it may not be one. A builder would not change the style of his building overnight because there was a new monarch on the throne. The house tells the story of somebody's life. Houses today are smaller because people do not work as servants now. The type of house depends upon the life style of a particular time.**

This pupil attended a school situated in a dull suburban backwater, yet the understanding and personal learning was extensive.

This use of the local landscape to develop an understanding of the past is practised in many other European countries. At the 1982 Nicosia Conference of the International Society for Education through Art, a Swedish teacher commented upon the success of a project based on Lerback, a suburb of Stockholm,

> And how the children drew! Many drew realistic responses to the architecture around them with a directness which showed the strength of their experience. These drawings form now the basis for our continued work with these children, following the lead of the questions they asked as they worked: what men wanted these carved (Baroque) doorways, who carved them out and how did all these people live, who fetched the water from the old pump in the square? Questions will continue to arise as they look, see, record and wonder.

Studies of the tangible remains of the past which are to be found in children's contemporary environment (eg a derelict and weed-infested lock) help them bridge the gap between reality (the canal) and the intellectual reflection which is a central part of the historian's craft. Since the remains of the past are in the child's own present, what better place can there be to extend experience than from the child's own position in space and time?

Buildings and artefacts have a past which is their own. Because they have a history, the past may be entered through a study of them. By becoming involved with these specific elements of a past, the learner (child and adult) is provided with a framework for study. Thus street furniture could provide the entry point ... or church furniture, window shapes or vernacular building materials. Many teachers are able to seize the ordinary and realise its potential in this way, as the following case study illustrates.

Case Study – Local History Study Unit: Inner city, street survey

Local studies provide a further dimension to family history for they explore a geographical area with which the children are already familiar. As with family studies, the group are not concerned with national issues but with the social, political, religious and economic fabric of the lives of ordinary people in the past.

In the study described below the teacher decided to concentrate on the search for evidence and the ways in which evidence, once collected, could be organised, evaluated and presented. The school was situated in a city suburb in an area which included Victorian housing, Edwardian terraces and post-1945 council estates.

Before introducing the topic to her class the teacher had undertaken some personal research:

1   A walk through the streets immediately around the school determined how best the area could be presented to children. Perhaps the main problem which besets every local study is that teacher and children think that they know the district well. Familiarity so easily breeds contempt! In her initial walks the teacher identified *and noted* such things as the types and ages of housing, buildings which had been extended or altered since their original erection, changes in the use of buildings (eg a chapel which had become a furniture store), date stones and plaques on buildings and on ironwork (eg the railway bridge), how land was used (for shops, housing, workshops, open spaces,

public buildings, parking, housing etc) and what land was
derelict.

This personal survey encouraged her to prepare a large
scale street map which clearly identified the area the
children were to study. This covered some 500 metres of
High Street and the roads and streets which radiated off it
– in one of which stood the school.

2   When the area to be studied had been clearly defined the
local librarian was invited to suggest what reference books,
maps, photographs and newspaper cuttings were available.
A selection was made and a stock of photocopied material
prepared to 'feed' to the class as the study progressed.

3   Maps were photocopied for each child – a modern street
map, and a map of the area as it was in 1938. Maps showing
the district in Victorian and Edwardian times were
mounted in the classroom, together with a small display of
photographs of the area in the 1910s, 1920s and 1930s.

The study was introduced through a slow walk along the High
Street during which time the children, equipped with clip-
boards, paper and pencils, were invited to note down anything
which would help towards a study of local history.

On return to school the material which had been gathered was
discussed. It included:

Dates eg Palmers Dwellings, 1874
          School Board for London, 1884
          Smith and Co., founded 1930.

Unusual *advertisements* painted on the sides of buildings –
'Virol, nursing mothers need it' prompted the enquiry 'Do we
have them now, Miss, nursing mothers and Virol?'

A *shield* on a railway bridge
A *pub sign* 'Queen Charlotte'
A *parish boundary* mark, 'St Phillips Parish, 1851'.
A *house plaque* recording that the house was once lived in by
an eminent doctor.
VR on a wall-mounted *post box*
A *coal hole cover* inscribed with the name of the manufacturer
and 'founded 1821'
A *boot scraper* outside a small cottage ('The roads must have
been dirty in those days')

A *gas lamp* on a wall stanchion
A *pawnbroker's* sign.

It was at this point, once the children had grasped the importance of careful observation, that the elements they had collected were analysed. The purpose was to try to decide what could be accepted as evidence of the 'built past'.

Dates seemed to give the children the greatest feeling of security. These were ordered and listed and the buildings to which they related written alongside them. Doubts were then expressed. Might not the date on a building only indicate part of its history? Did a date on a foundation stone *prove* that the building was completed during the year recorded upon it? Why did the school have two dates – one for 1884 and one for 1897? Identifying the dated buildings on their modern street maps was comparatively easy. Were the buildings also on the 1938 map and the maps of 1902 and 1880? This prompted the observation 'Some buildings sort of disappear as you go backwards from now' which led to the reflection that although the buildings may change, 'the land stays in the same place'.

The other collected elements were discussed in turn. Some, like 'founded 1930' were queried. 'It says 'Bespoke Tailors' on the shop sign, but they sell newspapers and sweets. It's still a shop but not the shop it was in 1930' (a remark which indicates an awareness of change in function over time).

The most difficult elements for the children to deal with were the pawnbroker's symbol ('My Nan calls that shop "Uncle's" '), the advertisement ('If it had a date on like for a pop concert you'd know') and the pub sign. Should we assume that the painting of Queen Charlotte meant that she had some association with the area? The question prompted two children to try to discover something about the Queen. (Her name, Charlotte of Saxe-Coburg Meiningen, stayed in their memories long after attempts to find any local links she may have had with the area had been abandoned.)

This initial looking and talking was an essential part of the study. It helped the children to realise that buildings were historical artefacts and thus evidence of a past (see Figure 3.7). As such they were legitimate elements to question. Figure 3.8 shows the children's questionnaire.

Figure 3.7 *Studying detail above a doorway – 11-year-old.*

Date of visit	23rd May 1990
Building	Jones (wool shop). Awal (newsagent)
Position	Corner, Wix St. and Ramage R.
	4 storied building.
Description	Yellow brown bricks for walls
	Slate roof
	Sash windows (lst, 2nd, 3rd floor)
	Large metal and glass windows for shop front
Date	Roof gable carving reads 1879
Original use	A pub? Below date carving which reads
	'Horse and Hounds'
Present use	1. Shop which sells wool, buttons, cottons
	2. Shop which sells sweets, papers.
Decorations	Two coloured brickwork
	Window boxes over newsagents shop
Things I noted	1. Satellite TV dish over wool shop.
	Someone must live there
	2. Burglar alarm and shutters on newsagents
	3. Coal hole covers in pavement
	4. 8 Chimney pots on roof

Figure 3.8 *Local study – Children's questionnaire (compiled on word processor)*

The purpose of the topic was to help children gain an insight into historical change over time, illustrated through the study of a residential area. It also provided a range of cross-curriculum activities. These took several forms:

1 Children were invited to *study a building* of their choice under the following broad headings.

a) *Materials* What materials have been used for the walls – brick, stone, concrete, wood? Do the walls have any form of cladding – stucco, tiles, weatherboarding? What materials have been used for the roof.

b) *The roof* What shape is it? Is it pitched or flat, hipped or gabled?

c) *Decoration* Is the building decorated in any way? Have the bricks been laid in such a way as to make a pattern?

d) *Windows and doors* What is the predominant shape – rectangular, arched? This led to book research on style.

Many of the terraced houses had Victorian Gothic door-
ways. The question 'Did a Gothic doorway *always* indicate
that a building had links with the 19th century?' caused
one child to suggest that 'perhaps you need more than one
fact to prove anything'.

2 *Analysis of the use of buildings* followed upon the question,
'What is the building used for today?'. This encouraged the
children to look at change over time: 'In the old photograph it
was a cinema. Now it's a Bingo Hall'. Physical evidence of
change was also sought, eg bricked-up windows, a new window
line, an extension built in materials which differed from those
used in the main structure. (It is worth noting that the backs
of buildings often contain more of the original features than the
fronts, an indication, perhaps, that owners have always wished
to present their 'best face' to the world.)

3 *Presentation of findings* The information which was collected was classified in a variety of ways. Pie charts were made
to show land use; maps were drawn to scale to chart each
'survey' walk; interesting buildings were photographed,
sketched, modelled. The teacher allowed each child to be
flexible in the way s/he responded to the experience.

4 *Contemporary issues* At the time of the study traffic
congestion in the area had begun to attract much attention.
The photographs of the 1920s showed horse-drawn transport in
the High Street. What changes, the children were asked, had
followed upon the ever widening ownership of the car? This
provided the opportunity to record how car ownership affected
land use – including the siting of a car showroom, a 'parts'
shop, a filling station and the provision of a car park behind the
library, garages in the council estate and the positioning of
traffic signs and parking meters. The teacher introduced the
idea that the parking meter might, one day, be displayed in a
museum, 'for everything has a history and is history'. This fell
largely upon unhearing ears, but simpler questions like 'How
did people move around without cars?' 'How long would it take
to walk from here to the nearest railway station?' prompted
enthusiastic discussion.

This kind of work provides a particularly appropriate entry
into the study of history because it builds upon knowledge

which the children already possess. Such knowledge, extended by looking and *seeing*, can be further deepened by the use of appropriate local archives (business directories, autobiographies, census returns) and the oral evidence of older people who live in the community.

Local studies can also be extended to include the parish church and its churchyard. Often the graves of generations of local families can be identified and linked to the houses or businesses which the children have been studying. This is particularly appropriate in rural areas where church burials have continued into the recent past.

The appropriateness of a local studies approach for children in the early years of schooling can be set within a broader framework. Local studies – whether in England or in Sweden – can only be used to comment upon a tiny fragment of a nation's history. They cannot give children any idea of the magnitude of the past.

Local studies, therefore, need to be set within a national (and international) context. To study the village of Coldstream in Northumberland will certainly help children develop an understanding of the people who were born, worked and died there in the 19th century. Yet it will tell them little of the industrialisation of the North of England. A study of Framlingham may lead to the uncovering of fascinating family trees; research on the tombs in the parish church; and an understanding of the hierarchy within the village as reflected by the housing and occupation of its inhabitants. It might encourage children to link visits to the castle with a study of life in Tudor times – of Mary Tudor, Lady Jane Grey, or religious persecution.

While such topics provide valuable experience and insight, they need to be set against a less parochial background. For the few weeks following the death of Edward VI what happened in and around Framlingham was politically significant. Implicit in 'coming to an understanding of a few weeks' is that the children will have been shown how to set these events against the national (and, if necessary, the international) scene. An analogy could be drawn with the town of Chernobyl in the Ukraine, before the nuclear accident in the Spring of 1986.

The death of Edward pitched Framlingham momentarily into the national consciousness, giving it a significance unheard of before or since. The centuries before these events and the centuries that followed upon them have been much less dramatic. It is all too easy for children (and for the writers of guide books) to concentrate upon the moment of history to such an extent as to cause the view of the past to become skewed.

The local environment can never provide a microcosm of the national scene. Indeed, unless carefully presented, local studies may confuse rather than clarify. The important aspects of life in a remote Cheshire village through the centuries may have little to do with the broad sweep of national history. Yet major national or international events will touch the village and change it. A memorial in church or village square will record the violent deaths of many young men in the fields of France.

Children need to grasp the continuous, subtle and sometimes hidden intertwining of the local, national and international strands which contribute to the study of history. They also need to understand that an event or development may have far-reaching implications, both geographically and through time.

The Bubonic Plague which ravaged Europe between the 14th and 17th centuries was international in its dimensions, spreading from the East Coast of China to the West Coast of Ireland within a human lifetime. In comparison with this example, the skill of paper making (also Chinese in origin) took nearly 1000 years to reach Europe. Both the plague and paper-making had effects far beyond the towns in which they were 'born'.

These reservations apart, local studies provide adequate material for small-scale study which will teach children method without swamping them with a spread of material which is too great for them to handle. Local studies are specific and have a low level of generality.

Like all the other approaches considered in this chapter, local studies should not be regarded as *the* approach but rather as one of several which, when related to each other, give coherence to the learning of history.

Strategies – local studies

1 Invite pupils to design a local trail to illustrate how people, over time, have built upon and shaped their environment. The trail could be presented as a map or as a notebook of buildings in an area. A modern tower block is as much an historical artefact as a Victorian cottage or a yeoman's dwelling built in 1450! The children can illustrate the notebook/trail with sketches, photographs and postcards.

2 Collect photographs and illustrations of the area immediately around school, both contemporary and historical. Discuss the changes which these pictures suggest. Can a picture be used to give a particular viewpoint? Can a photograph be biased? Are photographs and illustrations *always* neutral?

3 Children can make a study of the use of materials in local buildings. Attention can be directed towards the materials most commonly used for walling, rendering, and roofing, eg stone, brick, pudding stone, flint, daub, wood, clay, plaster, glass, slate, concrete, straw, tiles etc.
Such a study can be conducted at a number of levels:

- *Individual*: What materials have been used to construct my house, my block of flats? Why were they used?
- *Group*: What materials are most commonly used in this area? Do the materials tell us anything about local industry and agricultural practice, eg the use of clay/straw in Devon, the use of limestone in limestone areas (Oxfordshire to N. Yorks), the use of flint in E. Anglia, of wood in Essex? Do the individual houses/buildings tell us anything about the level of technology at the time of their construction? When were individual buildings constructed? What were they built for? Can we tell from the outside of a building how it is now being used? What might the inside look like? Has the building been altered since it was built? How do we know? How can we be sure?

4 Use Ordinance Survey maps (early editions can be purchased) to pin-point developments which may not be immediately obvious from walking around an area eg rerouting of roads, destruction of buildings, change of land use (eg agricultural to industrial or domestic, industrial to domestic or leisure)

5   If there is an old parish church near the school a study of the graves can provide evidence of such things as local occupations, family groups, life expectancy in previous historical periods etc. A grave survey also provides much statistical material for mathematical investigation and representation of findings through graphs and charts.

6   Imaginings (a group activity)

The activity below presupposes that the children have visited the site of a Roman Fort. The Fort is used as an example, but the activity can be applied to many kinds of historic site.

Give each group a map, drawn on grid paper, of a fortified Roman camp. On the plan, the children mark ditches, walls and defended gateways, barrack blocks for 300 soldiers (100 of whom are cavalrymen), a headquarters building with a shrine to Jupiter, cookhouse, toilets, store rooms, hospital and accommodation for the commander. What other features might need to be identified eg water supply, the geography of the surrounding land?

Try to base the plan on the Roman pace as the unit of measurement (a Roman pace = 2 paces).

Could the plan be explained through the use of Roman numerals?

Questions to explore

1   *Street names. What different words are used to describe 'street space', eg alley, court, garden, mews, square, terrace? Do they indicate how the space might once have been used?*

2   *Are some streets named after people or events? Why were particular names chosen?*

3   *What are the most important public buildings in your local area? What function do they perform? How long have they been used for this purpose?*

4   *If you were given a sum of money to save and rehabilitate one building in your area, which building would you choose to save and why? For what purpose would it be used in the future?*

5   *How much can you find out about the history of the local public services (police, ambulance, fire, coastguard, customs)?*

Looking at the local area – Teacher's checklist

School building	*Sources of information*
Building style	O.S. Maps (contemporary and historical)
Materials used	Local maps
Date built	Local newspaper reports
Surrounding area	Local Authority records
Within school perimeter	The school log book
	Oral – former pupils
	former teachers

Within 1 km	
Houses and apartments	Maps (as above)
Shops	Photographs and prints
Workshops	Church and chapel registers
Factories	Trade registers and almanacks
Garages	Census returns
Stations (bus/rail)	Reference library
Warehousing and storage	Local museum
Churches and chapels	Publications of Local Historical
Public memorials	Aids
Graveyards	County Archaeological Service
Derelict/waste ground	County Archivist
Public buildings	Local newspaper archives
Bridges and tunnels	Oral – local people
and, if appropriate	
Museums and wildlife parks	
Farms and agricultural buildings	
Archaeological sites	

Strategies – Training observation

These activities help develop close observational skills of the kind essential for 'seeing' changes in the built environment.

a) *Kim's game* Place a range of objects on a tray. Let the children study the objects for one minute. Cover the tray. Ask the children to write a list of the objects they can remember. The game can be varied in several ways:

• Begin with a few objects and gradually increase the number.

- Change one or more objects (eg a 5p coin with a 20p coin, a lead pencil with a coloured pencil) and invite suggestions as to which has changed.
- Move the relative position of two or more objects on the tray.
- Require that a list be written of specific types of objects or of objects which have particular qualities (eg objects that might be worn, objects which cut, objects made of metal).

b)   *The potato game*   Give each child in the group a potato. Request that each write a description of their own potato so that it may be easily identified when all the potatoes are displayed together. Extend the game by using other fruits, vegetables and flowers which have less individuality, eg carrots, apples, daffodil bulbs, onions.

c)   *The 'I know what it looks like' game*   Invite the children to draw from memory an object with which they are very familiar. Begin with simple objects (eg a bread knife) and move on to objects which are more complex (eg a pair of spectacles, a kettle, a step ladder, a pair of scissors, a bicycle). How accurate are the drawings? Could a person wear the spectacles, cut with the scissors, ride the bicycle, pour water from the kettle, erect the step ladder? These memory drawings can then be compared with drawings made with the objects in view.

Exercises of this kind encourage children to look carefully and to realise that personal accounts and impressions, however sincerely given and well presented (in writing, in pictures), should never be accepted unquestioningly.

History – a patch approach

'We did the Vikings. We've done Normans. I expect we'll do Tudors next. My sister did'

Tom, aged 9

The patch approach takes one small section of time past and examines it in some detail. The study will seek to show how people lived, the economic resources which were available to them, indicate something of their religious beliefs and social customs, how they spent their time (at work and leisure), where they lived. This broad framework (stressed in the four elements which are to be included in every historical study*) will also indicate something of the economic, social, political and religious pressures of the period under review. The Welsh child who has really become immersed in the life and times of the labourer or skilled artisan of the 1860s will be better equipped to understand the drift of population from Welsh village to English town. Feelings such as hunger, a desire to provide for one's children, helplessness cross both time and space. The following case study illustrates a patch approach using a computer simulator.

Case Study – Classroom based study unit

A simulation exercise

The topic – the Plague Year 1665 was based upon a computer programme and its accompanying desktop material. (1665. *The Great Plague of London*, published by Tressell Publications, 70 Grand Parade, Brighton BN22 JA). The disc had been prepared for young people in the 11–16 age range but it was also suitable for use in years 5 and 6.

The package consists of a pupil's guide and record sheet, a book of contemporary accounts of the plague and a teacher's guide which provides a wide range of information about London life in the 17th century (with specific reference to housing and health). From the outset the children, working in groups, were encouraged to study 'Bills of mortality'; the programme helped the children to interpret them and so obtain some understanding of how deaths were interpreted and recorded.

The visual display invited the children to refer to specific information in their personal guide/information book. This ensured that the context in which the programme had been set had been fully grasped.

The children then divided into working groups, each group representing a Public Health Committee responsible for a particular area of London (Aldgate, Bishopsgate, City Centre, Cripplegate, Eastcheap, Holborn, St Paul's, Southwark).

---

*The political; economic, technical and scientific; the social and religious; the cultural and aesthetic strands recommended for each of the National Curriculum Study Units.

Within each group each child assumed the role of a member of the Health Committee – for example a local Knight, Lady, physician, prominent resident. The groups met monthly throughout the Plague Year (although in the simulation exercise these monthly meetings could follow immediately one upon another!). Their task was to respond to the impact of plague and pestilence in the area for which they were responsible.

As the programme developed, statistics were fed to the group which indicated how the outbreak was spreading. The committee were offered a range of solutions which might ameliorate the situation. 'Do we take on an expert rat catcher and pay him 2p a rat? Can we meet this cost from the funds we have?' 'Should we pay for a hospital to be built or take over the local church? If we use the church whose permission do we require?'

Each member of each committee kept notes on each meeting, on a specially prepared proforma. As the programme developed the children came to realise that the decisions they made had particular consequences (not all of which could be foreseen). Thus the programme encouraged discussion and consensus and allowed the teacher to point out the contribution which individuals can make to the unfolding of particular historic events.

The danger of concentrating upon a patch approach is that the nature of history – change over time – can become lost in a series of leaps from one period to the next. As Bloch points out, human evolution must not be presented in a series of violent jerks. There is also the danger that when working in this way children enthusiastically crash into the past, taking with them modern values and contemporary attitudes. Discrimination does not come easily!

Strategies – a patch approach

1   Study one famous local person in depth, eg the person who is commemorated by a statue in the town square; a person who is buried under a fine tomb in the local church. Who was he/she? When did he/she live? What can we find out about his/her life?

2 Provide a newspaper (photocopy) which commemorates a significant event eg VE day. How much does it tell us about that day, that particular period in our history? Where else could we obtain further information? From other newspapers? From museums? From older people?

3 Examine entries in the school logbook over a one year period to build up an understanding of 'how this school once was'. Have adult attitudes to children changed? If so, how? Have schools changed – and in what ways?

History – a topic approach

'I want to follow a topic but I don't seem to be able to fit mathematics in.'

Student on teaching practice

The topic (or centre of interest) makes history a bridging subject linking a number of different areas of study.

A group of nine-year-olds visited a Tudor house near Lavenham in Suffolk. The experience (the visit) was used as a starting point for all manner of activities. They made accurate plans and drawings of the house, from which they built a scale model (mathematics, art, craft). They had discovered at the house a map showing that in Tudor times the area was heavily forested. They tried to estimate how much wood had been consumed, how it might have been used and how land use had changed as a direct consequence of deforestation (ecology/land utilisation/mapping).

The children learned of Tudor 'personalities' – of Drake, Queen Elizabeth, Walter Raleigh, William Shakespeare. They plotted Drake's voyage around the world (geography); acted Pryamus and Thisbe from *A Midsummer Night's Dream* (drama); and followed Tudor cooking recipes (maths, home economics). They created Elizabethan costumes (craft and design), sang madrigals, read the poetry of Herrick. They wrote to the National Portrait Gallery for Tudor portraits, they visited the village church to find Tudor tombs. Their involvement became so total that it was impossible to classify their learning within clearly-defined subject boundaries. The approach gave unity to content and the message which shouted from the classroom walls was one of excitement, discovery and enthusiasm.

We might be tempted to ask whether history as a discipline becomes lost when such an approach is adopted. This is a question which might be echoed by the mathematician, the geographer, the teacher of religious studies or the scientist. Is knowledge for the primary child a unity and should we seek, through integration, to remove from subjects their distinctive quality?

The difficulty of presenting a structured subject-centred approach will be known to most teachers of young children. The great majority of eight- to ten-year-olds with whom I have worked have been able, at a rudimentary level, to distinguish between subject disciplines. They are usually aware, for example, that history is different from geography, that science examines areas which are not found in religious studies. (Although they do not necessarily have the knowledge to say how they differ.) Nevertheless it must be apparent that in the primary years children have not had the opportunity or time to acquire the range of background knowledge that is essential to them before they can be expected to embark upon an academic study. It is impossible, for example, to talk about the voyages of discovery of the Vikings or of Vasco de Gama without some appreciation of the seas, oceans and continents.

Young children need to be exposed to a variety of ways of looking and ways of thinking (as well as a variety of ways of responding). It is this which demands of primary teachers a particular, non-subject-specialist response. The teacher in Chesterfield who tries to recreate something of the atmosphere of 18th century England by introducing her class to the painting of Gainsborough, the poetry of Blake, the music of Handel, a story based on the life of Lincoln, with visits to Chatsworth and an industrial museum in Sheffield, is strengthening and enlivening the place of history in the curriculum.

When the broad context has been established and understood, children can be led towards an analysis which might follow an established academic procedure. As Dewey observes:

> 'Abandon the notion of subject matter as something fixed and ready made in itself, outside the child's experience as something hard and fast: see it as something fluent, embryonic, vital and we realise that the child and the curriculum are 2 limits which define a single process. Just as two points define a straight line, so the present standpoint of the child and the facts and truths of studies define instruction. It is a continuous reconstruction, moving from the child's present experience out into that represented by the organised bodies of truth we call studies'[4]

The academic steeped in his/her own specialism and way of working may find the implications of this observation difficult to accept. Yet Dewey counsels caution. Both the educator absorbed in child-centredness and the academic seduced by a subject-orientated approach need to be made continually aware that no one method will do all that is necessary to give a child understanding. How easy it is 'to seize upon something in the nature of the child or upon something in the developed consciousness of the adult and insist upon *that* as the key'.[5]

Strategy – Topic and theme

Construct 'trees' of the type shown in Figures 3.9 and 3.10 for each topic/theme you wish to develop. These can be used as the basis for illustrating the way in which elements within a study overlap. The plan designed for a study could be photocopied and distributed to each child in the group, or used as a wallchart which can be referred to during teaching/classroom discussion (see Figures 3.11–3.13).

History – a line of development approach

> *'They had no toilets in those days!*
>
> > *Mary, aged 6*

The 'line of development' is perhaps the most widely used approach in teaching history to primary children. In it a specific element is taken – for example, the wheel, transport, how people lived, costume, our town/village – and used as a peg on which to hang particular historical periods. A history of 'The house' might take a class of nine-year-olds from cave to tower block in ten easy leaps. The pictures and reference books used for such a study may well be chosen with great care. Nevertheless, concentration upon one central element tends to narrow the perception of the children undertaking the study. The development of the house is not just a matter of more skilled building methods. Technological advances (eg the development of a means of mass-producing glass), an improved transport system allowing building materials to be moved cheaply across the country, the availability of cheap capital have all influenced and affected the development of the house. The medieval

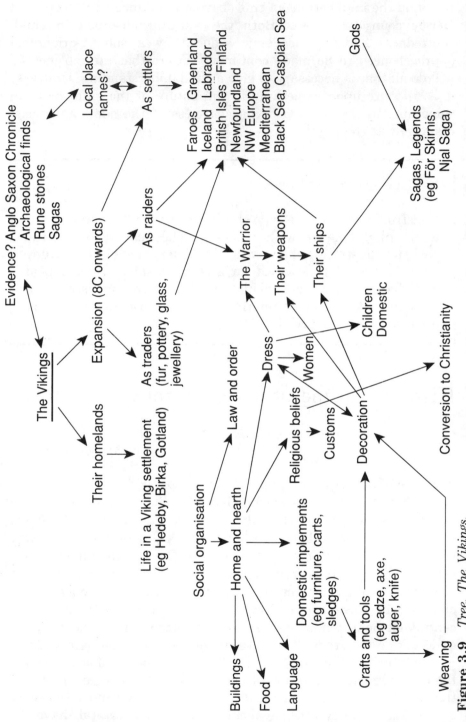

Figure 3.9   *Tree. The Vikings.*

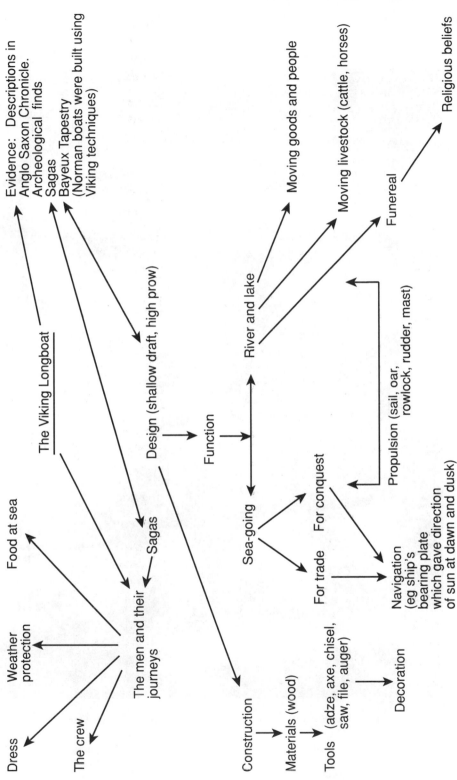

Figure 3.10 *Secondary tree, The Viking longboat.*

Figure 3.11   *Display on 'The Vikings in Britain' (Nine-year-olds).*

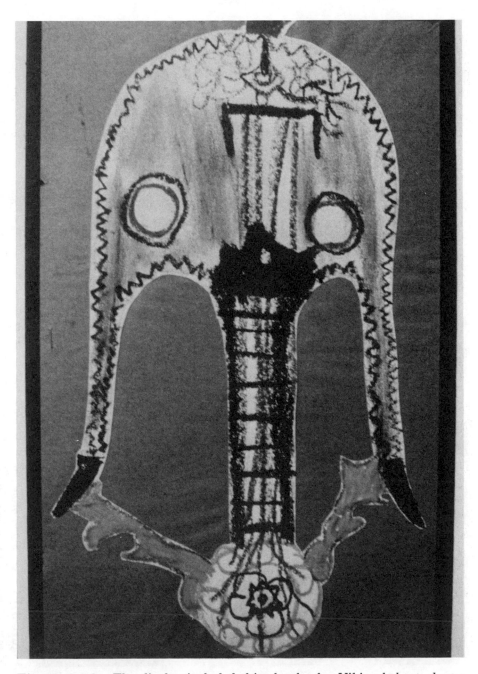

Figure 3.12 *The display included this sketch of a Viking helmet, drawn on a museum visit. (Eight-year-old).*

Figure 3.13 *An imaginative painting called 'Invaders'. The Saxons are the tiny figures on the left, the helmets represent the advancing enemy. (Ten-year-old).*

moated house was not suddenly replaced by Tudor hall and then by Jacobean mansion. The gradualness of change, the inter-relatedness of the social, economic, industrial and political threads which make up the life of any community can be so easily ignored with such an approach. This tends to happen when the approach to history teaching – through a series of short halts in a rapid move through time – diverts teacher and taught from the more considered approach which characterises, for example, an in-depth study of the development of the village, town centre or local railway line.

Presenting history in terms of the development of one particular artefact (eg the sail, the oar, the wheel) can easily skew a child's understanding of the past, for there is the implied suggestion (when this approach is unthinkingly adopted) that the artefact *in its present form* marks accomplishment, success. It is all too easy to apply contemporary values to the past and judge success and failure, good and ill, in twentieth century terms. The study of houses or costume through the ages has value for young children because these are topics with which they can identify. But the people living in the homes of Stuart or Hanoverian England or wearing the dress of a Welsh miner at the time of great depression had values and attitudes of *their* time not ours.

Strategies – Line of development

Approaches through a line of development will require continual reference to classroom and personal timelines (see pages 24, 26–27).

Reference to linear development in history relates most satisfactorily to very slowly changing elements in human development, eg the recording of numbers, the subtle changes in the meaning of words and the historical roots of colloquial and folk sayings. A fascinating explanation of the slow evolution of the English language is to be found in Dorothy Hartley's *The Land of England* (Macdonald, London, 1979).

The importance of a varied approach

Each of the classroom and school-based approaches considered above has something to commend it. Done well, local studies, family history, the project, the theme and the topic, can help children to develop a sense of time past, foster the growth of historical imagination, encourage reflection and go a little way to establishing 'what it is to be an historian'.

With young children this will be best developed through people, the things they did, the artefacts that they used. Too often the people selected, though worthy and significant, are adults driven by adult needs, desires, aspirations. Throughout our work in schools it is important to remember that a child's view is often less cynical than our own. Discussing whether Charles I was wise to allow Stafford to be executed, Mary, aged nine observed 'Why did Pym not make Stafford promise to go and live in the country and forget about governing. I've got a father and I wouldn't want him executed. Surely Parliament would have understood ...' It is not only contemporary values that have to be side-tracked when looking at the past but also childhood perceptions of the world. And yet this beautifully simplistic approach to the harsh reality of political life contained a germ of hope. Mary suggested an alternative to execution, another way, a speculation 'perhaps if only ... then things would have been different'. The suggestion considered by the group, that the size of Stafford's Irish army might have been multiplied by his enemies, also raised the issue of truth and half truth. 'We know he died on the block. Was it right to kill him? Did Parliament have the facts? Do we have the facts now?'

This richness of response was not the consequence of following a particular approach, a singular method. It came about because Mary and her friends had been exposed to the past and were encouraged to talk and discuss their ideas about it. History for them was much more than writing adult-processed facts into notebooks.

References

1   Lewis, Bernard *History – remembered, recovered, invented* Princetown University Press USA, 1976, p 11.
2   Ballard, M (ed) *New movements in the study and teaching of history* Temple Smith, London, 1970, p 93.
3   Pluckrose, Henry *Seen Locally* Methuen, London, 1989.
4   Dewey, John *The School and Society* University of Chicago Press, 1910, p 11.
5   *ibid* p 104.

4 Learning history – beyond the classroom

If the purpose of history teaching (to quote the Schools' Council guidelines) is to deepen children's understanding of their world, to widen their experience through the study of people of a different time and place, to appreciate the process of change and continuity in human affairs, to think critically and to make judgements whilst *at the same time* acquiring leisure interests[1] then visits (well prepared and researched by the teacher) must occupy a central place in the school curriculum.

If met, the broad conceptual and philosophical expectations set out above would in turn make more specific demands upon the children. To make *effective* use of a visit to a castle (like Warwick), a yeoman's cottage, a reconstruction of the past (like the Ryedale Folk Museum, Yorks), a conventional museum (like the Maritime Museum, London), an experience museum (like Yorvik), or a working museum (like Beamish) will promote the development of both concepts and skills.

History through visits

It is evident that teachers and museum curators accept that children learn from the combination of a total experience as well as by focusing upon individual elements within it. The Roman tile offered to children in Newport museum, the medieval dagger handled by groups of nine-year-olds visiting the Museum of London serve to whet curiosity, provide a framework for discussion and give opportunity for a degree of personal synthesis and understanding. The following case study shows how the study of a single object can be developed.

Case Study – Exploring an artefact

A group of nine-year-olds handle a medieval pot. They pass it from hand to hand, feeling its texture. Some even smell it . . .

Informally the museum curator asks them questions; the questions are multidimensional and open ended. Their purpose seems to invite the children to reflect on human links with the pot, its use, the person who made it.

This is an object from our collection. Look at it, touch it, smell it if you like. Perhaps you might like to close your eyes as you touch the rim. Try to make your hands see ...

- *What do you think this is?*
- *What material do you think it is made of?*
- *What do you think it was used for?*
- *How old do you think it is?*
- *Who do you think may have made it?*
- *How is it decorated?*
- *Does the decoration tell you anything?*
- *How big is it? How heavy?*
- *Does its size tell us how it might have been used when it was in everyday use?*
- *Who might have used it ... somebody rich? somebody poor?*
- *Where might they have used it?*
- *Where might they have kept it?*
- *Was it manufactured or made by hand?*
- *What tools might have been used to make it?*
- *How can you tell?*
- *Do you think a lot of these were made?*
- *Was it valuable when it was made?*
- *Is it valuable now?*
- *Is it valuable to an historian/archaeologist? Why?*
- *Has it been mended?*
- *Why do you think it has been repaired?*
- *This pot was found in three pieces in an excavation in the centre of the town on the site of a merchant's house. Why do you think it may have been thrown away? Why do you think it survived?'*

The talking is followed by a short period of research, firstly in the museum where other pots are displayed against a range of commonly used 15th century artefacts. Once set within a context, books are passed between the children containing more pictures, additional information.

Only then do the children begin to write and draw.

Through the provision of concrete and tangible forms of evidence, children can be helped towards building up a picture of the past as historians. This is essential if concepts are to be developed, for they 'cannot be acquired by prior prescription, only built (upon) extended, relevant experience.'[2]

Before becoming seduced into thinking that visits provide the resolution to the conceptual difficulties which young children face when studying an academic subject such as history, it is important to reflect upon the quality of the experience offered. Indeed any inappropriate or ill-prepared visit can be as destructive of interest and understanding as an ill-conceived lesson based upon a poorly-written textbook.

It is also important to remember that children immersed in any museum-based activity, are seeing and handling only the *relics* of a human past, not that past itself. The artefacts represent evidence upon which the children can draw to deepen their understanding of what was. Such items can never be a vehicle to transport learners into another age. That said, museums occupy a central place as guardians of the artefacts from the past and as such have a significant role to play in the education of young children.

The success of a visit to a museum or historical site should not be measured in terms of the number of worksheets completed per child or the hours spent on the site. Indeed it could be argued that *of themselves* worksheets are educationally worthless, encouraging children to adopt the view that answers to facts are the very stuff of history. A museum can provide a setting in which the remains of a past can be displayed, talked about, touched, wondered over. But history itself cannot be directly inspected. History is concerned with how people behaved, why they behaved as they did and the events which precipitated or followed upon their actions.

Too often the worksheet is allowed to become the key to the visit, its completion marking the end of the experience. Too often the questions themselves are closed (and thus conveniently markable), and encourage little reflection or self-questioning. Too often they direct the children's eyes to the things *which the worksheet planner* feels to be significant. In my experience children are much more likely to see if they are encouraged to look for themselves. Visual literacy cannot be taught through typed sheets of A4.

On a more fundamental level the 'closed' worksheet reduces the children's need to look at the artefacts themselves. The answers often lie in the labelling, so the child ignores the source and instead concentrates on an interpretation of it. Activities like these consume the time available but do little to develop in the learner any understanding of the nature of historical enquiry.

Fines argues that worksheets which prompt a 'Le Mans' style start' followed by a race to the finish, demean the experience itself and reflect ill upon the respect we should show to children. For the less able, they are potentially disastrous!

> Visits (should be) seen to be learning about valuing. They are being asked not just to see something rare and special, but also to respond to the experience. Valuing is a high level skill, yet we should not exclude it from the major aims of education simply because it is difficult.[3]

Strategies – visits

Visiting a museum

Before taking children to a museum consider what knowledge they are likely to acquire and how this will fit into the work being undertaken at school. It is always advantageous to be familiar with the museum to which children are to be taken. Many museums provide source material for use by school groups. But beware! Museum worksheets may not fit the needs of every group and their thoughtless distribution and use could produce a negative response.

1 Prepare a questionnaire which relates specifically to the period and the elements within it which are being studied. Wherever possible, design questions which are open-ended and which require more than one word answers. The questions should encourage a variety of types of response – prose, poetry, drawings, charts, diagrams.

2 Give time and opportunity for individual children to respond in their own way to artefacts which appeal particularly to them. This implies that a short period should be set aside, whenever appropriate, as a time for 'personal looking' and it is also important that the results of that looking be valued by everyone.

The poem which follows was written in such a setting by 10-year-old Graham. In a museum case he discovered a small metal horse which had been made as a sacrificial offering to a pagan god. It moved him to write:

Horse

Horse made of metal
Horse with twisted tail,
Horse made for sacrifice
How many he has seen
I cannot tell.

Horse with thin tummy
Horse with long neck
Horse with small head
How much his eyes have seen
I cannot tell.

3   Divide the class into small groups of four or five children. Invite each group to discover and record objects made of specific materials. For example, in a Viking exhibition they could record artefacts made mainly of wood, bone, base metal (specific and/or general), precious metals and precious stones, clay, leather, natural fibres, stone, glass, bone and horn.

On returning to school invite groups to explore how these objects relate to each other and comment upon the period under review. What do they tell us about the development of technology, for example, or the skill of craftsmen and women? (If a more recent period is being studied the list given above can be extended to include artificial fibres, paper and card, and plastic.)

This kind of activity will encourage note taking. Each example will need to be supported by a note of what it is and its 'given' date.

4   Invite pupils to design a guide book (this could be an individual or group activity). 'Imagine a friend is going to come unaccompanied to see this exhibition. Prepare an illustrated guide for him/her to follow. You may need to include a simple map (showing where the museum is situated) and a room-by-room plan.'

5   Class reference book. Before visiting the museum divide the class into small 'study groups'. Each group will concentrate upon a single element within the exhibition – clothing, entertainment, weapons, food, housing, occupations (crafts?), children. On returning to school give each group an opportunity to mount a display of their findings and to discuss them with their classmates. Finally elements from the displays can be incorporated into a class study book.

6 It is worth enquiring whether the museum provides handling trays. These are collections of artefacts relating to a particular period. The objects, when handled, can become the medium through which the life of human beings of the past is recreated. Physical contact adds a new dimension to experience.

Visiting an historic building

The introductory remarks to 'visiting a museum' are equally relevant.

1   The guide book/building trail. Invite each child to design a trail to illustrate interesting aspects of the building/site. (See museums strategy 4.)

2   Study a portrait or family group. Invite children to study the picture carefully and recreate the pose of the person/people in the portrait. Does the pose adopted tell us anything about their attitudes, beliefs or place in society. If a group picture is used, do the poses adopted hint at the relationships of the people in the portrait?

3   Design a museum shop related to the historic site the class have visited. Invite the children to make a list of the things it should contain and to justify their selection.

4   Encourage the children to design a 'talking' museum/house guide for a person who is blind or partially-sighted. What things would it be appropriate for them to touch? What is the best route around the house and gardens? Invite the children to reflect whether the items and areas they have selected will help the blind listener to better understand the history which the tape seeks to explain. Could sounds (other than the human voice) be included?

Problem solving

Problem-solving activities in which children are invited to make decisions within a set of specific restraints of place and time have become a central part of many on-site visits.

a) 'You are the Constable of this castle. You have 40 men at arms. You are about to be attacked by a force twice as large as your own. What defensive measures would you take? Where would you place your defenders? Would you try to defend the whole site or part of it?'

b) 'You have been ordered by the King to attack the castle and free two of his Knights. Survey the castle and try to discover its weakest spots then plan an attack. You have twenty men to help you.'

c) 'You are a servant. Your family priest is hiding in the house and government agents are searching for him. What part of the house might safely be used to provide the priest with shelter? Design a safe route which you could use to lead him, at night, to freedom.'

NB *Each of the activities described above will need to be related to a particular site and a specific period in history.*

d) 'You are an estate agent who is acting on behalf of the owners of the property. They wish to sell. Write a description, setting out the property's particular characteristics and its elements of specific historical interest. You may wish to support your description with a drawing or photograph and a poster.'

e) 'You are a TV director. Choose two rooms and six objects which you will use on your programme to show viewers the most interesting historical aspects of the property – and encourage them to visit it themselves.'

f) 'You are the head cook. You are told that 20 important guests are to arrive tomorrow evening and will need to be entertained. What plans will you need to make? What food will you serve?' (This activity could be undertaken by a group of children, each child focusing upon a different historical period to show changes in diet, living style etc.)

g) 'You are the local Lord and have just heard that the Court of King Henry Vlll is to stay on your country estate for three days. You decide to oversee the entertainment – the musicians and dancers will need to be instructed in how best to present a masque of which the King will approve. What programme do you prepare? Remember it may rain!'

h)   'Write an advertisement (eg for a Cook/Parlour maid/ Gardener/Butler/Ostler) for the house you have just visited. Set the advertisement in a particular period. Remember that to do this you will need to find out what the work involves and what wages should be paid. Is your servant to live in the house? Will a uniform be provided? Can someone apply who is married?'

4   Photography (black and white and colour). Encourage children to make a visual rather than written record of their visit.

5   Tape. Encourage children to tape an interview with the owner, administrator or warden.

Invite them also to try to capture sounds which can be used later to 'evoke' memories of the visit (Fountains playing in a walled garden, the creak of a staircase or floor boards, the shutting of a dungeon door, wind on the battlements).

Handling materials

1   Not all children will have had the experience of touching/ handling materials which are referred to in history texts, historical fiction or in excerpts from diaries and autobiographies. A handling box containing a range of objects and fabrics can help redress this. The box could contain such things as a glazed pot, an earthenware dish (biscuit fired), a wooden knife, a wooden dish, a piece of pewter, scraps of sackcloth, silk, velvet, woven piece of wool, raw wool, a sharpening stone, a flint, an object made of iron.

2   Children can be invited to undertake a handling exercise similar to that described in the case study in school.

a)   Invite them to ask questions about an everyday contemporary object, eg a chair

b)   Provide more obscure objects for them to question, eg a flat iron, a last, an old tool, a piece of jewellery, a hat pin, a wartime identity card.

Checklist – Visits

Has the visit succeeded in:

- Deepening understanding of classroom-based work?
- Improving the children's handling of information – through their interpretation of written and spoken word, pictures, dioramas, artefacts, guidebooks, reconstructions, film, video and sound recordings?
- Helping children to build up 'wholes' from fragments (eg the possible direction of a castle wall between two towers) through observation and intuition?
- Showing children the relationship between function and structure eg What do you think that this might be? How might it have been used? Where? When? What is it made from? Do we use similar things today?
- Improving the children's ability to relate a range of artefacts one to another and to the people who made them and setting them within chronological time?
- Developing different forms and styles of recording – in words spoken and written (descriptive, creative, analytic), photographs, drawings, models, maps, charts and diagrams?
- Developing the children's historical imagination and understanding of what it might have been like to have been alive at some time in the recorded past?

History through re-enactments

A group of nine-year-olds are sitting on a wolf skin. They are roughly dressed in furs. Their arms, legs and feet are bare. In front of them kneels a man, bearded, his body stained and grimy. The skins he wears are held together with cords made of fibre. By his side is an axe, its stone head tied to the rough wooden shaft. In his hands are two flints which he hits together. He chants, almost inaudibly. The children seem to be wondering 'Will the fire never come?'

This example is taken from a re-enactment organised co-operatively by a museum and a primary school. It is a typical recreation of the kind which is being used to help young learners imagine 'what life might have been like'. The key to the success of historical enactments is the degree to which children become involved and manage, for a brief moment, to displace time. The happening described above was set in a clearing in a small wood, close to the museum. When the weather prevents the use of the wood the 'happening' takes place indoors and much of the atmosphere is lost.

In England the National Trust has been amongst those pioneering this way of working. In 1977 a Theatre-in-Education company was established by the Trust. Between 1977–1984 over 75 000 children have taken part in 'performances' (re-enactments) in the Trust's properties throughout England and Wales. It is worth outlining the key elements in the programme.

Each programme involves up to 70 children who work with five or six actor/teachers and an actor/musician. Several weeks before a 'performance', teachers of the participating schools attend a briefing session at which a pack of source material is distributed. This contains background information to the event or happening, instructions on how to make costumes and accessories, and music for children to rehearse.

On arrival children are divided into small groups working closely alongside one character (actor/teacher). A plot (known to the 'core' company) develops. This takes the children – by now role playing – into the house and grounds. The 'characters' encourage the children in their group to make their own decisions and to participate in and lead the action. The children are encouraged to see an event through the eyes of a particular character and to use these varying interpretations of an event for discussion and follow-up work on their return to school.

Historical re-enactments are also organised by the local education authorities, by Education Officers working within national collections (eg The Tower of London) and by private institutions (eg Kentwell House, Long Melford, Suffolk).

The purpose of the re-enactment (and the time devoted to it) can be justified at several levels. First, the quality and nature of the experience seem to make it much easier for children to recall historical information and to comment upon it.

They cut the wood in a saw pit. The person in the pit was the underdog. He got all the sawdust in his face. Perhaps when he became the person on the ground he would remember how hard it was to be underdog for hours on end.
(Ten-year-old)

It could be argued, therefore, that re-enactments seem to have a much bigger impact upon children than do more traditional methods of teaching. As one south London primary school teacher observed to me: 'I believe wholeheartedly in giving children experience. I took a class of 4th year juniors to Carrisbrooke Castle. They explored the building, dressed up in armour and relived the past. It gave them experiences on which to discuss castle building, methods of attack, methods of defence. When we returned to school the class even made siege machinery'.

Second, the re-enactment can become a vehicle through which children are brought face-to-face with historical evidence. In Glasgow the National Trust were allowed to acquire a tenement house of 'outstanding insignificance'. It had been lived in by one person during late Victorian and early Edwardian times. He had one endearing quality, he never threw anything away. In this house children are invited to enter the past by encountering material which will provoke questioning and research.

The success of any re-enactment depends upon the choice of site and/or period and upon detailed preparation. The enactment *in itself* is but a coming together of a wide number of inter-related activities. Children will need to be encouraged to research a wide range of background topics (clothing, food, lifestyle) and to become experts in a tightly-defined historical period (requiring knowledge of specific people and particular events). In the process they will become aware of the problems of the people whose lives they are recreating. (How long did it take to travel from London to Devon in 1829? What route was the quickest and least dangerous? Did it make any difference if the journey were taken in February or in June?) Before the re-enactment happens the children taking part will have read books, leaflets and charts, written notes, looked at maps, made drawings and models, collected photographs, taken rubbings from ironwork, brickwork and memorial stones – for all personal and group activities serve to provide the foundation upon which the re-enactment will be built. Put simply, the 'event' provides a means of uniting the curriculum through the purposeful and appropriate application of its component parts.

Re-enactments need not be confined to the museum or the stately home. In the school in which I worked a group of 9- to 11-year-olds researched – with the help of their teachers and other knowledgeable adults (like grandparents) – the way in which air raids affected life in London in 1941–42. Visiting museums, listening to Vera Lynn, and delving into period newspapers resulted in a costumed musical review of the period, attended by parents in costume as well as teachers and children. (see Figures 4.1–4.3) The observation that 'children could never have invented war. It's an adults' game' from a 10-year-old boy indicated that the dressing up and singing had in no way encouraged him to regard war as anything but evil and unnecessary.

A teacher in a school in Kent told me how her class of 10- and 11-year-olds became fascinated by a model of the *Mayflower* which had been brought into the classroom by a child who had made it at home. The interest the model generated led to a detailed study. The children delved into the background of the families who went on the voyage. This led to children playing the roles of the heads of the families when they met to discuss and plan the journey. They discussed the voyage *as though it were in the present.* To do this they needed to have a detailed understanding of the context in which it was made . . . the desire for religious freedom, a world of expanding frontiers and of indifferent communications.

The questions posed and discussed were practical and appropriate. The journey to the New World – was it possible? What human, personal problems would need to be faced? How could the frightened and the undecided be reassured? What equipment and provisions would be needed? Might they fail?

The children drew the deck of the *Mayflower* in the playground. The families (36 people in all) stood within the deck space to see how cramped they would be. They then wrote an imaginative logbook which recaptured the inconvenience of life on board, including the smell and the noise. They described the fury of the storm which forced the *Speedwell* to run for shelter. As the teacher observed, the simple re-enactment helped the children to understand that the Pilgrim Fathers were real people who felt pain and anxiety!

Re-enactments, inside a museum or outside it, encourage children to participate, to become active learners rather than passive onlookers. We should remember, however, that activity *of itself* (activity which has no clearly-defined goal) has little to commend it. Dressing a child as a Roman, a Viking or a wartime Cockney could be regarded as educational window dressing unless the child has been helped to feel and come to know the tensions and expectations of the times that are being re-entered (Figure 4.4).

'It was amusing to wear Stone Age clothes' is a typical twentieth century comment. If the child travels home in them in the back seat of the car the value of the enactment may be reduced to nothing –

Figure 4.1 *A re-enactment which linked school and community by focusing upon a period of history which drew upon oral sources – evacuation and the Home Front . . . .*
- *through drama . . . .*

Figure 4.2 • *through painting . . . (six- to eight-year-olds)*

Figure 4.3 • *through displays of artefacts supplied by parents.*

Figure 4.4   *Sensitivity to period. Children from Cornish schools experience an Edwardian Christmas in the 'Big House'.*

an unnecessary and spurious dressing up. It is worth the time and effort to let him return to this century in his own clothes.

Recapturing the past in this way requires certain skills of the teacher. These might be listed as:

- a clarity of vision (a realisation that those taking part need to have the appropriate contextual framework in which to move)
- a sensitivity to the period being investigated
- integrity and respect for the material upon which the enactment is to be based
- awareness of the arts which characterised the period being studied (dress, music, poetry, architecture etc)
- awareness of the technology that contributed to the production of buildings and artefacts
- the ability to communicate – both to the children taking part and any onlookers – that what is taking place is more than a conventional dramatic representation in which actors move in a planned, predetermined way.

As we saw in an earlier chapter, empathy is the ability to imagine oneself as another person in another time and place and thus to relive another's thoughts and feelings. This means that the enactor must have both a wide contextual understanding of times past and an understanding of human nature at a fundamental level. Is it likely, for example, that a seven-year-old could 'get beneath the skin' of Alfred after his defeat by the Danes? And how superficial the role play becomes if it is reduced to a playlet telling of a poor housewife and her cakes!

This means that at primary school level, effective role play will be possible only if sufficient background material has been prepared within the classroom and understood by the class *and* if the group as a whole have the maturity to cope in some depth with the complexities of human life *at an adult level.* In responding to the predicament of Buckingham, impeached by Parliament, a class of nine- and 10-year-olds became so deeply involved in the re-enactment (which took place in the Tower of London) that the arguments for and against his impeachment (and execution) continued throughout the journey back to school. The discussions were wide-ranging and reflected wide differences in the children's levels of understanding.

Let him go. He has children.
Why execute a man for following his King?
He is guilty. If freed he will return with his Irish Catholic army.

> **Impeach Buckingham. Yes! The King will then be easier to control.**
> **Parliament is jealous of him because he is the King's friend. The charge is (one of) spite.**

Children who take part in well-prepared re-enactments are given a high level of experience to which they can respond. Perhaps this is all we can hope to provide. The texture and climate of each age permeates its contemporary society. Religion in the 17th century, political radicalism in the 19th, the impact of technology in the late 20th, all shape and influence the people living at the time. Young children are unlikely to be able to grasp such subtleties. If they are unable to do so and take instead their own prejudices and expectations into an enacted past, little will have been achieved by the exercise.

This major reservation notwithstanding, children can be helped to develop historical understanding from patches of personalised experience. For young children the 'humanness' of the past, experienced on a small individualised scale may provide a route to understanding. The Viking frying-pan with the food still stuck to it (Yorvik site, York) points to the fact that the Vikings, too, were human ... that Ulla had the same problems when cooking an egg as they might have had.

John Hodgson, sometime Education Officer of the National Trust, described to me how this human dimension can spring from an enactment in which evidence is taken and examined. He quoted the programme developed by the National Trust at Killerton, Devon. The children undertake studies at school which centre upon slavery, the work of the Clapham Sect (Wiliam Wilberforce, Henry Thornton) and the effect of their findings upon Sir Richard Acland (who lived at Killerton).

The children then visit the house where they become involved in a 'happening' which actually took place. At the house they meet a group of MPs who have made the journey from London to persuade Sir Richard to give money to support the anti-slavery campaign. Lady Acland opposes this expenditure arguing that the money would be better spent on founding a school for the village children. The gardener, Beitch, wants the money too; he aims to improve the gardens and argues that taking on more labourers would reduce unemployment among local people.

The discussion, in which the children played a full part, demanded that the children left the present and relived through their imagination an event from the past. They were taken into the discussion by the actors and were expected to comment upon the arguments which were advanced and to make suggestions of their own. The dilemma they were resolving *was* of the past yet it touched upon issues which are central to political decision making today. Do we put finite resources into the Third World, into a social service (like education) or into infra-structure (like clearing local rivers and improving the draining of pasture)? The groups taking part were helped to realise that men and women have always been faced with such decisions.

In re-enactments of this type the actors have a crucial role to play. They are not history – they are alive now. They are not from the past. Like the children they are players, moving into the past from the present. Their first task is to take to themselves the feelings and attitude of a past age, to feel appropriate to and comfortable in an age which has gone. These feelings and attitudes, hopes, fears and expectations they must then project into the present. In so doing they become the sounding board against which children's ideas are explored and developed. The actors do not shape the children's responses. Their task is to ensure that the responses will fit easily into the 'texture' of the period which is being studied.

Significantly, as John Hodgson pointed out, the final decision was left to the participating children. The freeing of slaves (the decision we might think children would find most appealing) proved no more popular than the provision of a local school, or the improvement of the squire's garden. When the groups returned to their schools more material was supplied indicating how the problem of the distribution of the money was actually resolved. This again provided an opportunity to talk through the similarities and the differences of the arguments which had been advanced and to look at elements which might have led to a particular decision being made. Has society's view of slavery changed? How did people regard slavery at the time of Acland, Thornton and Wilberforce? What sort of society was it that could buy and sell men, women and children? Where did the slaves come from? How were they transported? Where were they taken? Did the West Country port of Bristol *really* grow from the trade? The teacher of history, interested as s/he is in origin, causal relationships, the sequence of events, the manner of change, the way men and women enact with and reshape their society and their successes and failures in doing so, has a rich opportunity through an example of the type described above to develop in young children something of the nature of historical thinking.

One important element in the example must not be overlooked. All the children taking part were given a clear contextual framework within which to work. They were also given evidence, although some of it was presented in 'second hand' dramatic form (and therefore open to misinterpretation both by the actors and by the children who look on). To the evidence they brought their own experience of life which, though limited, was nevertheless relevant. 'How would you behave in these circumstances?' – a question directed at an individual child, brings a human response. Provided a number of relevant and contrasting situations can be created in the primary years, children can be led to appreciate that history is about human beings and that knowing what it is to be human helps them to 'guess' at how people *possibly* behaved (under given circumstances) in times past.

In passing, it is worth nothing that these 'dips' into the past, provided they become a regular feature of the life of a primary school, fulfil Bruner's requirements of the spiral curriculum. Well researched re-enactments whether within school or outside it, can provide children with the opportunity to move from the simple and the concrete to the complex, comprehensive and abstract through a graded sequence of representations. Moreover the academic disciplines which underpin history are much more likely to be understood if each child is actively participating by doing, seeing, feeling; by using spoken language; by listening and actively responding to words and sounds. Implicit in all of this is that the teacher must be aware of what he/she hopes to establish as a result of the experience. Re-enactments in which children take part simply as entertainment or light relief from the daily classroom chores are likely to be counter-productive.

Strategies – re-enactments

1 Establish on-going links with such bodies as the local museum service, local historical societies, the National Trust Education Department. Such links will provide information about future activities – in which re-enactments of some kind will possibly feature. If children are to take part the school history programme can be directed towards providing appropriate contextual material.

2 School and class based re-enactments need to be well organised and sensitively planned. They provide an appropriate way of celebrating school anniversaries, eg 'Our school, then and now'. Source material could include such things as extracts from old logbooks and registers, photographs, local newspaper reports, material from LEA archives, DES, Ministry and Board of Education reports and circulars, interviews with former pupils (recent and those long left) and appropriate materials from local diaries and autobiographies.

3   A re-enactment can be undertaken by an individual class eg a class within a school could follow a 'Victorian school day'. This would require the classroom to be made as formal as possible with few pictures on the walls and a minimum of equipment for the children to use. The day could begin with the recitation of The Lord's Prayer and a thanksgiving for Queen and Empire, followed by Bible Reading and religious instruction, writing on slates, reading primers, chanting tables, working sums, a spelling test and drill. The headteacher (or well-prepared parent) could visit the class and take the role of visiting inspector. Such an experience is made more memorable if all taking part are appropriately dressed for their part (including the adults!).

The 'experience' can also take in playtime, with the children playing appropriate games eg hopscotch, skipping, jacks, marbles, hoops, tops, two balls. Lunchtime provides a further opportunity for 'reliving the past' with the children eating the kinds of food which would have been taken to school for 'dinner'. Obviously this will necessitate further research, for the food eaten should be appropriate to the area and also reflect the social status of the children who would have attended the school. The greater the consideration given to such minutiae, the more effective and realistic will be the end result. A 'Victorian' child who brings food to school in a plastic bag is an example of the kind of anachronism we should seek to avoid.

History – drawing upon 'sense of place'

It seems to me that children learn most effectively when all their senses are harnessed. I have therefore long held the belief that atmosphere is an important element in the learning process. And yet 'atmosphere' when related to a young child's understanding of history is difficult, if not impossible, to define or analyse (see Figures 4.5–4.7).

Figure 4.5   *Creating atmosphere*

Figure 4.6 • *morris dancing* . . . .

Figure 4.7 • *pancake races . . . .*

Douglas McMurtrie points out that today's world is technically sophisticated, functional and lacking in aesthetic appeal. He argues, however, that:

> There is within us a bottled up emotional area waiting for release if we are to become fully human, yet it has been denied an opportunity for expression: the subjective perceptual way to understanding is no less respectable than the scientific.[4]

McMurtrie develops his argument to show how little those of us who teach allow intuition and sensitivity to play a part in the learning process. He demands that we find time to allow children to experience historical sites and ruins, for each evokes a 'feeling of the impact of history upon the living'.

A church tower standing windswept on a Norfolk heath ... Fountains Abbey ... Stonehenge ... may cause the mature adult to stand, stare and wonder.

But, it could be argued, such monuments are unlikely to evoke a similar response from a seven-year-old who has no historical framework into which to fit the experience. Is Stonehenge anything more than a few old stones, a tower in a field anything more than something to climb?

To write about 'feelings' and 'atmosphere' is perhaps unusual. I realise that I am moving from the cooly academic into an area unsubstantiated by research. Words like 'feelings', 'atmosphere', 'wonder' and 'alive' suggest a personal response, a response which will vary through mood, circumstances and association. Yet we ignore and debase the humanness in children if we deny them the ability to wonder, reflect and marvel. The group of nine-year-olds who sat with me in the dungeon of Norwich Castle whilst the door was locked, the light switched off and the jailor's steps took him (and his keys) to the daylight and fresh air above, shared, for a few brief moments, a dimming of the present. We were not surrounded by spirits of the past – to think so would have been fanciful. But we knew that other men and women had sat there, just like us. For them, there was an uncertain end; for us the 'jailor' would soon return to take us back to the present.

This example, which led to much reflection on crime and punishment 'then and now', might appear to have been too contrived. Let me therefore link it to another incident which occurred at Fountains Abbey, lit by floodlight on a calm, quiet, late summer evening. The response to this experience by a nine-year-old was, 'Stand still. You can almost feel the monks'.

These two examples, inconclusive in themselves, suggest that children are able to make imaginative leaps and that imagination can be triggered by place, sound (or silence) and circumstances. Place, sound and circumstance in combination can fuel wonder, even awe.

Ralph, aged eight, climbed the twisting stairs which lead to the top of the tower of Ely Cathedral. As we reached the top it began to snow heavily. 'Imagine', he said 'being a builder, up here, in winter'. On returning to ground level, the group (seven- to nine-year-olds) began to discuss the possible ways the tower was built. How did they do it? Did they have cranes? How did they cut the stones? Did they have scaffolding?

Place, sound, smell and circumstances do not of themselves deepen historical understanding. They are not even peculiar to history. One can wonder at a tree silhouetted on a hillside against the setting sun. Yet each of those elements which are encompassed by the word 'wonder' can lead to a deepening appreciation of what was, of humanity's struggle against the elements, of primal fears and anxieties, of what might have been.

It may well be that children who are invited to question what they see and to wonder at it, keep this quality throughout their lives. 'What is it? Why is it there?' are not specifically historical questions. But the answer to 'why is it there?' will inevitably lead to 'when was it put there/made?' 'By whom?'. In responding to the questions and observations sensitively we are helping to construct a framework of time and place against which later experiences can be set. It is not always necessary to begin with an historical context: the context and a deeper understanding of it, often grows from the experience.

I am not alone in believing that a personal response to atmosphere deserves to be respected and built upon by the teacher (irrespective of the age of his/her pupils). Its value and significance are stressed by Hodgson. He writes:

> First we must encourage adults to see that sensitivity to atmosphere has some value; then we need to persuade ourselves that it is better to receive what a site offers for itself than to give a free rein to our own preconceptions of what it ought to be offering.[5]

Put another way, he observes:

> Old houses are full of spirits which long to speak to us if we are receptive enough. Of course it is difficult to hear if you are one of 30 children in a school party, if you have already been conditioned to

reject those strange messages part of your mind is receiving and if the teacher has her own idea of what you are to learn from the experience.[6]

To allow a child's imagination free rein when thinking about the past will not produce an historian; neither will children continue to be interested in history if their natural curiosity and inventiveness have been crushed under a score of dates and un-noteworthy lives of long-dead Kings.

We must not allow ourselves to be trapped by one method, one approach, one teaching style, one sort of text book, one kind of presentation. To be effective we need to be able to harness almost as many approaches as there are children in our group and to acknowledge the personality and subjectivity of each of our pupils.

Strategies – a sense of place

1 *Atmospheric writing*   Invite children to write, sitting in the house, on the castle walls, in a dungeon, within the quiet of a cloister. By writing on site children are less likely to write pieces which begin 'We went to Fountains. I sat next to Jenny. We both had an ice cream'.

2 *Listening*   Whenever appropriate, build into a visit a 'listening time' when the children, perhaps only for a minute, sit motionless and listen to the sounds which pervade the site. Even if there are few sounds, 'listening through silence' is a worthwhile activity!

3 *Reflection*   What is special about this place? What mood does it convey? Does the building/site/ruin suggest anything of its original purpose? (Questions one could ask of Stonehenge, the ruins of a fortified house on the Northumbrian moors, a church shell on the site of a now deserted Norfolk village.) Is it possible to imagine a particular event happening here (eg Queen Elizabeth's visit to Kenilworth). Does the site speak of the past?

4 *Photography*   Give children the opportunity to photograph an unusual element which captures the past – the face of a monk on a capital, an overgrown medieval trackway (like Peddars Path in Norfolk), the worn steps to a monk's dormitory, the weatherbeaten bricks of a Tudor tower, the adze marks on the beams of a timber cottage.

References

1　The Schools' Council *A new look at History*, 13–16 Project, The Schools' Council, 1976, p 12.

2　Rogers, PJ *The New History* The Historical Association, London Pamphlet 44, 1978, p 34.

3　Fines, John Unpublished paper *Principles of Educational use for sites of special quality* delivered at Goodwood Symposium, Sussex. March 1985 (written October 1984) See also: *Teaching History* Holmes McDougall, Edinburgh 1983.

4　McMurtrie, Douglas 'Landscape with ruins' *Environmental Education* Winter 1984/85, p 10.

5　Hodgson, John *Reaching the parts which other methods cannot reach* National Trust, Education Department, Laycock, Wiltshire, 1985, p 2.

6　Hodgson, John *ibid,* p 1.

5 Planning – elements for consideration

The position which history enjoys as a foundation subject within the National Curriculum has implications for each teacher and for every school. In its narrowest sense it places a responsibility upon teachers that the children in their care will be helped to acquire knowledge and develop the concepts, ideas and skills which are central to the study of history. Fortunately the expectation is much more ambitious than this.

The 1988 Act requires that the curriculum 'promotes the spiritual, moral, cultural, mental and physical development of pupils at the school and of society' and 'prepares pupils for the opportunities and experiences of adult life'.

To meet this and to ensure that the curriculum is coherent, balanced and broadly-based it is intended that the links between the core and foundation subjects should, wherever possible, be emphasised. These cross-curriculum elements can be presented in a number of ways:

- cross-curriculum *dimensions* – personal and social education, multicultural education and equal opportunities.
- cross-curriculum *skills* – literacy, oracy, numeracy, study skills, representational and recording skills.
- cross-curriculum *themes* – environmental, economic and industrial topics, citizenship.

For these curriculum strands to be developed in a coherent way and to minimise inappropriate repetition, the school staff will need to establish a school policy for each core and foundation subject, continually bearing in mind the importance of the ways in which subjects interrelate. For example it is almost impossible to help children grasp the significance of the voyages of Columbus, Cabot or Drake without some reference to the contemporary level of technological development in ship design and navigational instruments, the primitive nature of cartography and the religious climate which shaped their thinking.

It therefore follows that before the curriculum can be planned a number of decisions will need to be made. These may be listed as follows.

1   Curriculum approach

How shall we present history in school? Should it be approached by concentrating upon concepts and skills (in which case agreed areas of content must be identified) or through a chronologically-based year-by-year scheme in the teaching of which an understanding of the concepts and skills central to history will be developed?

Within these two approaches the methodology followed will vary from school to school and from class to class. Some schools may decide to adopt a programme in which history is subsumed within a broad topic or thematic programme, some may use history as *the* subject which gives meaning to other studies by providing the vehicle which enables them to be set in a context of time, place and circumstance.

Even these decisions will be coloured by where the school is situated, for location affects our perceptions. A school in Totnes, surrounded by the evidence of a medieval past, provides staff with quite a different historical environment around which to plan children's learning than that offered by a school in a decaying inner city.

This local dimension has even greater significance when consideration is given to the particular nationality of pupils. For example, there has always been a Welsh dimension to history which has been appreciated by Welsh teachers but not always by textbook writers. The implications this has for the presentation of history to children whose background is not white, Anglo Saxon and Christian are of considerable significance. How do we present British colonialism in the 18th and 19th century? How do we explore such topics as slavery, the Crusades, British 'heritage'? Such difficult areas cannot be ignored, but require sensitivity to the pupils' cultural backgrounds.

2   Curriculum planning

How will the history curriculum be planned and which member(s) of staff will be responsible for overseeing the implementation of the scheme? Such a question may cause the reader to smile a little sadly! Most schools are too small for there to be a clear delineation of responsibility on the basis of 'one teacher, one subject'. Nevertheless, implicit in the National Curriculum is the requirement that each school develop a strategy for subject delivery. It may therefore be the case that in small schools each member of staff is made responsible for a 'basket' of subjects, eg English/drama/performing arts; history/geography/religious education; science/design and technology; mathematics/computing skills; music/drama/art; physical education/dance and movement. The divisions suggested here are quite arbitrary and depend upon teachers' subject strengths and interests. The groups outlined above are only possible if there are at least six teachers on the staff who are able and willing to undertake the considerable reponsibilities inherent in such an arrangement. There is always the danger that when particular curriculum responsibilities are assumed, undue specialism may lead to a lessening of the cross-curriculum elements which help give meaning to young children's learning and do much to enlighten individual subjects.

However the curriculum of a school is developed, regular planning meetings (See Chapters 7 and 8) need to be held to review the way in which core and foundation subjects are developing and the directions in which each can relate to the others both in general and specific terms.

One particular area which will also need to be addressed is the suggestion by HMI that attempts should be made to achieve greater continuity between schools, and the recommendation that Primary and Secondary schools co-operate more fully. Some schools have established planning groups made up of teachers from neighbouring infant, junior and secondary schools. The purpose of these groups is not to standardise the history curriculum but to try to ensure that children are offered a coherent programme and that the curriculum in each school is compatible. It is hoped that this will avoid unnecessary repetition of work undertaken.

3   Resources
Central to the implementation of decisions about methodology and content is the use of resources. How resources are shared between competing curriculum areas is a matter for the staff of each school. However there are resources peculiar to the teaching of history which need to be identified:

a)   *The local museum*   Try to discover whether the museum holds collections of documents and artefacts which relate to identified areas of the school curriculum. Some museums also organise an educational loan service. Are there facilities within the local museum which could be used by groups of children on an extended basis? Are there staff in the museum who would be able to contribute to historical topics undertaken at school?

b) *Local societies* (Historical Society, Civic Amenity group etc) Local people, particularly those who have lived in an area for a length of time, are often a rich source of information. Approaches made 'officially' through the secretaries of local organisations will often reveal an untold wealth of specialist expertise. (Drawing upon my own teaching experience I could list the retired archeologist who specialised in the Roman period, the treasurer of a steam railway preservation society, a museum artist whose life work was to create whole objects from fragments, a father who was delighted to share his model-making skills on the construction of early aircraft and ships.)

c) *The local library* Links established with the library will enable titles to be obtained which are specific to particular topics being taught and allow a wide range of books to be provided for the children's use.

d) *The local Planning Authority* The Planning Office of the District or Borough Council can often be of help by providing such things as lists of scheduled buildings and large-scale maps (for which a photocopy fee may have to be paid). The Authority may employ a Conservation Officer who might be persuaded to give talks in school and to supply information about buildings of local significance.

e) *The local Archeological Unit* keeps records of all historical sites. These units are responsible for all periods of history up to and including the nineteenth century. The Unit can be contacted through the office of the local council.

f) *The County Record Office* Information about original documentary sources is obtainable through the County Archivist. Search facilities are often heavily booked and it is wise to make an early appointment if photocopies of documents are required for class use.

g) *National organisations* which have been established to encourage an appreciation of British history and heritage, eg The National Trust, English Heritage, The Civic Trust. Each of these organisations has an education department and publishes materials which can be used in the classroom (see Useful addresses, p 180).

h) *Local sites* Links should also be made with professionals responsible for historic sites in the area, eg schools in Portsmouth or Middlesborough might contact a shipyard; Coalbrookdale is close to schools in Telford; a mining site might be approached by schools near Camborne.

One method of ensuring that the material collected is not lost is for it to be indexed (perhaps on floppy disc) and stored centrally. This means that a school can slowly acquire its own archive of booklets, pictures, maps, slides and tapes. One school in which I worked built up, over a period of some ten years, a comprehensive collection of historical maps and pictures. Stored in large envelopes in a chart chest they were roughly grouped by period, with specific envelopes within each period devoted to such things as building style, costume, local and national events, home life.

4 Book provision
Decisions on book choice are to some extent determined by the curriculum which is to be implemented. Do we choose a textbook per child per year group from a series adopted for the whole school? Do we choose individual titles for class libraries and a limited number of books from sets for the school library? Book resourcing is such an important consideration that it merits a short chapter of its own (Chapter 6).

Within the classroom – a personal checklist

The decisions taken at school level will be realised within each individual classroom. Perhaps the simplest and most effective way of focusing upon historical studies is to reflect upon the 'messages' conveyed by each classroom. Obviously the age of the children will determine the amount of time and space given to history, but an examination of the following key areas provides a basic framework for self-assessment.

a) *Displays* (see Figures 5.1–5.4) Do displays of the children's work comment upon the work undertaken and indicate a level of historical thinking appropriate to their age and ability? Do the displays include examples of imaginative, discursive and empathetic work as well as straightforward accounts ('Yesterday we went on a bus to . . .'). Is written work supported by models, paintings, maps, diagrams, photographs and books? To what extent have other curriculum areas been tied into, and become part of, the historical study?

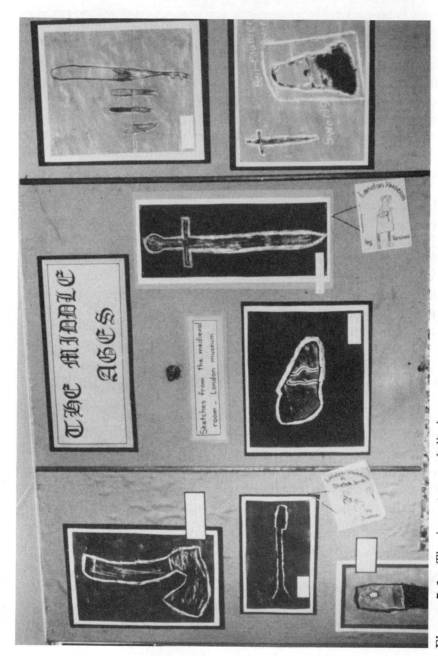

Figure 5.1   *The importance of display*
• *six-year-olds* . . . .

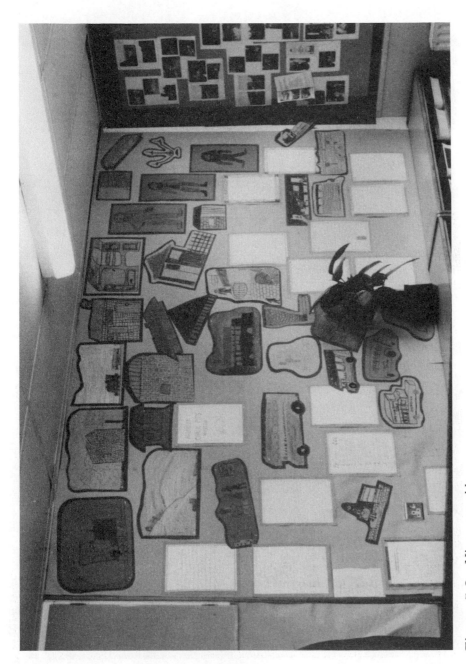

Figure 5.2 *Nine-year-olds.*

Figure 5.3   *Ten-year-olds.*

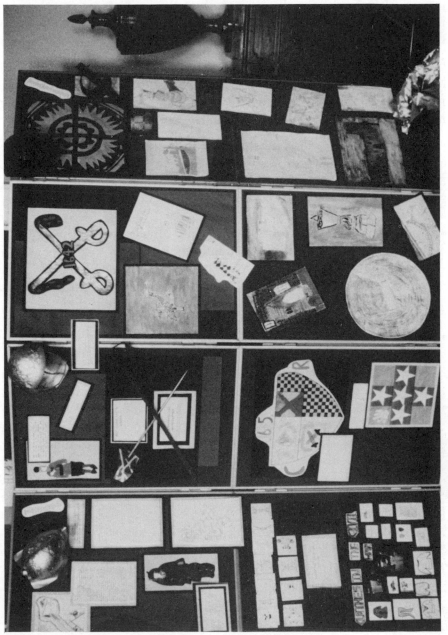

Figure 5.4 *Ten- and eleven-year-olds.*

The visual impact of the room needs also to be set in the context of what the classroom walls were 'saying' last week and last month. To what extent do the displays change to proclaim new areas of learning? Does the weight given to humanities, science, mathematics and language change imperceptibly through the term? How can the displays be regularly changed to reflect this shifting emphasis?

b)   *Time line*   Is the time line used regularly – not only for history but also for other disciplines eg the life period of a writer, scientist, mathematician, musician, artist. 'Beethoven was alive and writing music when this was happening in England . . .'

c)   *Class museum*   This need not be an ever present element in the classroom. The museum need not be large – a small table on which a number of artefacts are displayed will invariably prompt discussion and comment. The 'museum table' could take several forms:

- *ephemera from the past* eg a Victorian ginger beer bottle, a large key, a wartime identity card, a bobbin, a book, a toy, a decorated tile. What can the children find out about each object? How might they then be labelled? What information might the labels include? How much of the 'discovered' information is factual, how much is assumption or guesswork?
- *theme collection* eg old toys; photographs of the area; posters; trivia (bus tickets, football programmes, guide books); postage stamps. A museum table of this type could be planned and displayed by individual children or as a group activity.
- *work-related exhibition* A museum table could be related to a specific visit, 'happening' or group experience. In the school in which I worked the parents and classroom auxiliaries made, over a period of years, a wide range of accurately researched historical costumes. These were used both for school and classroom drama projects and as centre pieces for 'museum' displays within the classroom.

A personal analysis of one's own classroom can be extended by a quiet appraisal of one's personal teaching style. Elements which might be examined include:

a)   *Stories, myths, poems* and other listening material (eg music, drama on tape and on TV). Do I use all available opportunities which allow for children's historical understanding to develop? Do I try to balance story periods in such a way that children are given the chance to listen to historical fiction, as well as to stories of fantasy and everyday life?

b) *First-hand experience* Is the programme designed so that children are given the opportunity to understand the nature of historical evidence, by being exposed to it in all its forms? Do children have the opportunity to touch artefacts, explore a site, question experts, experience oral history? Is the curriculum delivery as varied as it might be?

c) *Resources* Does the classroom have sufficient resources available for children to record their experience in a variety of ways, eg through paint, pencil, tape, disc, photograph, model making, mapping? Which resources need supplementing when finance is next available?

d) *Timetabling* Does the historical experience offered to the children provide space in which they can explore their ideas through the *spoken word*? How successful am I, the teacher, in opening up possibilities of historical enquiry which might not be immediately obvious to the children? 'Might the princes in the Tower have been murdered by Henry VII? Why might he be happier with the princes dead?' 'Why do you think that Florence Nightingale found it difficult to gain support for her idea of taking women as nurses to the Crimea?' 'What might have driven Elizabeth Fry to devote her energies to prison reform?' 'How might Ghandi have felt on learning that troops had fired on a peaceful civilian demonstration, causing many deaths?' 'Cranmer died for his religious beliefs. Do people have such strong personal faith today? Why was Cranmer prepared to give up his life?'

Time for talking is a timetabling priority. Discussion gives children the opportunity to use language in a variety of ways – to describe, to explain, to explore ideas, to question an observation, to reflect, to comment and hopefully, in a historic sense, to speculate.

e) *Cross curriculum links* (This has been touched upon throughout the preceding chapters.) How effectively do I build cross-curriculum links into the teaching programme? How well are they being sustained? This responsibility will parallel that of purely teaching history, for it should be part of nearly everything we do within the classroom.

f) *The classroom environment* This, of course, embraces all of the elements touched upon above. The structures provided will hopefully be sufficiently relaxed as to encourage experiment yet sufficiently rigorous to stimulate intellectual growth. This will most likely be achieved when teaching strategies are chosen to meet short-term objectives (eg sequencing) as well as the long-term goal of 'learning what it is to be an historian'.

The curriculum which is eventually designed by individual schools must perforce broadly follow a form approved by the Curriculum Council. To this extent the content is prescribed and the freedom of the teacher restricted in the way in which core units are presented. However, scope for initiative remains in the school-designed units of local studies.

6 Using books

With ink anyone can write anything
A squire of Lorraine, commenting on a dispute with his local monastery, 11thC.

The Russian poet Yevtushenko begins a poem called *'Lies'* with these lines.

'Telling lies to the young is wrong. Proving to them that lies are true is wrong'

His attack was not directed specifically at teachers but at society, which so often presents half truth as truth and possibility as certainty. It is because history, well taught, encourages questioning that it behoves all who work with the young to select with care the printed material which is presented to them. The problem which we have to overcome is that the material which we all-too-often present to young children has frequently been filleted and pasteurised by the author (as a writer of textbooks I cannot deny guilt by association!).

History teaching is of little value if all that we do is to further the notion that there is an inherited and accepted knowlege, a body of indisputable facts about the past which need to be memorised. We should therefore seek to avoid using material which directs children towards a predetermined end. The example which follows is taken from a textbook published in 1921. Today it reads amusingly, but the message it conveys was probably unquestioned by the teacher who used it, the children who memorised it or the society who accepted it.

The ruling classes proved to be just as selfish as they had been before. Rome was growing more idle and pleasure loving. England is strong and prosperous because she has a wonderful middle class who bring prosperity through industry and commerce, a middle class often called our backbone.[1]

In Western society we seem to have elevated the printed word above all other forms of communication. This makes it difficult for children to decode or to evaluate the information that books contain. Indeed, for the great majority of children, their background knowledge is so slight that it would be an impossible task to invite them to do so.

It is for this reason that we who use (or write) the printed text need to do so with great care. If, for example, we choose to follow a chronological text, how are the selected periods defined and why have they been chosen? Is it because the writer seeks to present certain periods as having more significance than others? Is a particular event chosen because (in the writer's opinion) it marks a milestone on the road to modern society? Is there not a danger, if such an approach is adopted, that history becomes little more than a superficial canter from past into present?

Such an approach is unlikely to encourage children to move away from the stereotyping which has for too long bedevilled our teaching. Although it might be argued that the crude stereotype provides 'a starting point for genuine historical exploration'[2], such a stereotype has to be refined. At a time when racial and national prejudice is reflected in much of contemporary society, teachers must at least try to ensure that the books which children use are neither biased nor patronising. Western culture does not represent the only view of civilisation. Unsophisicated cultures are not necessarily lacking in grace or riddled with savagery.

Despite these reservations the school history book can provide a rough framework through which children begin to develop a sense of the sequence of history, 'those real events in time past into which new information can be fitted'[3] Carefully written, it *can* provide something of the nature of history, the study of the flow of time past to time present. It *can* provide an introduction to the language of history, the grammar used by the professional historian.

Thus our yardstick when choosing or using any book which gives historical information should be based upon an awareness and understanding of the concepts which are central to any study of the subject. Furthermore, it could be argued that there should be a far greater range of text/information books in school and classroom bookshelves than they usually contain. Nine- and ten-year-olds are capable of referring to adult books. Burnshill's *The Vernacular House in England* (Faber), a standard adult architectural study, deserves a place in the junior school library alongside books written specifically for children (eg *The Book of the House* by I. Carpi (Benn) or Molly Harrison's *Homes in Britain* published by Allen and Unwin). The availability of a range of printed material inevitably allows the presentation of different viewpoints. Their very presence – particularly if several viewpoints are regularly offered – will encourage children to ask questions.

Another approach is to use stories and legends to comment upon, explore and vivify historical studies. Often stories for younger children begin with the words 'Once upon a time . . .' or 'Long, long ago . . .' They go on to tell of a person in the past, a fictional child, a real man or woman who had an adventure, overcame a difficulty, achieved their goal after many trials and tribulations. The story, well told, (be it legend, fiction, fact or fantasy) helps children to become reconciled to the realities of the human condition, that man and woman, boy and girl, have throughout time had to face common and, therefore, shareable problems. We can imagine through our own sharing of the human condition (though we cannot 'know' in a historical sense, for we have no evidence to support such a claim), that it was probably just as painful for the child of a peasant family in the France of the Bourbons to be made parentless by war, disease and famine as it is for a child today in South Africa, Sudan or Namibia.

Thus stories, well told, can be used to reflect the minor changes in human circumstances, 'the expression of an unchanging human predicament' and 'the joys, sorrows, hopes and fears of mankind since the beginning of time' which Oakeshott sees as central to the study and appreciation of history.[4]

I would argue most strongly that in the early years of schooling, the story provides the ideal vehicle for helping children acquire an interest in the past. It allows children to become something of a traveller in time, to comment upon the story from their own position in time and also to move into the story and interpret the events within it through the eyes of its principal (time–imprisoned) character. This approach – be it through simple biography or through the lives of more legendary figures – allows children to build up a sense of time past.

It is within this story framework that children (of 8, 9 and 10 years) are likely to meet (at an intellectual level with which they can deal) some of the central issues of society past and present. What makes a good leader? Do events in the life of Nelson help us understand the nature of leadership? How are decisions made? What made the men of Kent converge on London in 1381? Can a crowd make a decision? Does an individual have rights? Were the Germans right to execute Edith Cavell in 1916? Is it reasonable to criticise the French for the sinking of a Greenpeace ship in New Zealand? Can the rights of the individual ever be greater and more important than the rights of the Nation State?

Yet such stories need to be chosen with care. How much better might life in Northern Ireland be today had the prejudices of the past never been fed into generations of Catholic and Protestant. In such a setting myth replaces history, legend becomes truth. The school, unwittingly, provides the bridge by which yesterday's historical legend becomes a model for tomorrow's real-life martyr. It is for this reason that revised texts are being used in some schools in the province – texts which seek to give a broader balance than has hitherto been the case.

The central place occupied by books and printed material as vehicles through which knowledge is transmitted to young children is a reflection of the part that the printed word has played in the development of Western society. Contemporary children (like adult students) are less book-bound than their predecessors. Ways of obtaining knowledge about the past are not confined to the printed word. Archive films, televised and taped discussion programmes featuring people who lived through an event, photographic material which extends the understanding of a passage of history are readily available and can easily be fed into any school's programme (be that programme locally or centrally controlled).

Understanding of the past is also developed in young children almost imperceptibly. The television programme which tells of today's events (be it specifically for children or for adult viewers) comments upon the here and now. Today's actuality is tomorrow's history. The media continually refers back to past events, to consider causes, and reflect upon possible effects; this, together with the visual impact of much of the film used, inevitably allows today's children to acquire a broader, less insular view of their society than (for example) was open to me when I was young. (To use the wireless well, one needed a facility with words. In my childhood the radio was little more than a speaking book.)

The immediacy and the richness provided by visual stimuli of the TV screen, can never replace books. What it can do, and has done, is to provide a jolt to those of us who teach. Imperceptibly, subtly, we have come to adopt strategies developed by the mass communicators. The development of film, TV and radio has coincided with a period when teachers of young children are reassessing approaches to learning. It is not surprising to discover that teaching techniques have developed to make the best use of the ever-increasing amount of technology which is available.

Strategies – book provision, years 3 to 6

Classifications

1 *National History*   One group of titles (in school or class library) should concentrate upon the broad sweep of national history. Such a series will present history as a continuously unfolding event, presenting the reader with a basic map of historical time. More than one series should be made available so that children can be encouraged to compare and contrast the different emphasis and interpretations which can be given to a particular event.

2 *Historical themes*   A second group of titles should be available which relate to topics and themes which can be studied within an historical framework, eg transport, iron, discovery. Such texts can be valuable if their use is restricted to clarifying studies already underway. If, however, they are used to foster the 'leap-through-time' approach, and the central discoveries in the world of science, technology and design which allowed the 'leap' to happen are ignored or superficially glossed over, such texts demean rather than enhance the teaching of history.

3 *Local studies*   Here the emphasis of the texts should help children develop a topic or theme and study it in some depth (eg castles, housing, my village).

4 *International history*   History is not only about the study of a national, ethnocentric past but also about the past in other parts of the world. Books should therefore also be available which relate to the great cultures of the past – Egyptian, Greek, Roman, Chinese, Inca. There should also be texts which relate directly to the cultural and ethnic backgrounds from which groups of children within the school are drawn – Afro-Caribbean, Asian, African, Irish, Chinese etc – and to British culture seen from abroad.

5 *Historical fiction, poetry and ballad.* Select texts which directly relate to the study being undertaken and the reading level of individual children. Children's writers who have

specialised in historical fiction include Joan Aiken, Nina Bawden, Peter Dickinson, Leon Garfield, Cynthia Harnett, J Meade Falkner and Rosemary Sutcliffe.

6 *Reference* This grouping would include specific reference texts, eg historical dictionaries; historical atlases of England and of Europe; titles particular to the district in which the school is situated, street maps of a town or district, books on local industry; books on place names, surnames, books about local people; local guides.

Choosing books

All the books which find their way into a school library should meet certain basic criteria. These could be listed as:

1 *Credibility and integrity* They should reflect current academic thinking and help children to grasp something of the methods adopted by historians in their study of time past.

2 *Depth and vision* They should help children appreciate that the world is made up of many cultures, that these cultures have a history of their own and that contrasting cultures can and do co-exist. What level had civilisation reached in China when the people of Western Europe were discovering bronze or when the inhabitants of Britain were erecting stone megaliths?

3 *Appropriateness of language level and content* This will be determined by individual teachers and directly related to the children they teach. Content will be shaped by national and local guidelines and reflect the policy of individual schools (eg local history studies, the adoption of a humanities programme of which history is a part) and by where the school is situated.

4 *Ease of use* Reference books offered to children should be 'user-friendly'. The links within chapters (and between them). cross-references and illustrations should be comprehensive and comprehensible. There should be evidence that the writer has been aware of the 'implied reader' when preparing the text and that this goal has been supported by the publishing house. Injudicious choice of typeface and unnecessary visual clutter can detract considerably from the impact of a book, although what it *says* might prove of great interest. If children are discouraged from decoding the message by poor presentation, its value is much diminished.

5 *Readability* All of the factors touched upon above will influence the extent to which a book is used. All books for children must adopt a style which relates to the likely level of understanding of the implied reader. Schools which cater for a wide age range will therefore need to provide books which reflect this fact – both in language reading level and intellectual expectation.

References

1 Newman, JB *Beginner's Ancient History* Harrap, London, 1921.
2 Watts, DG *The Learning of History* RKP, London 1972.
3 *ibid.*
4 Oakeshott, Michael *On History and other essays* Basil Blackwell, Oxford, 1983.

7 Reflections on content

Nowadays, the cultural heritage is seen to consist not only of the great artistic and monumental manifestations of human history, but also of all those elements that constitute a point of reference for a community. These factors do not operate independently, but interrelate with one another within a new integrated concept of heritage, covering historic landscapes, traditions, artistic manifestations and archaeological remains to form an homogeneous whole.
European Centre for Culture, Barcelona, 1990

The outlines included in the working party's document for the National Curriculum[1] indicate clearly the areas of study which are to be studied, together with the four elements which are to form a central part of each (Political; Economic, technological and scientific; Social and religious; Cultural and aesthetic). The order in which the units are followed and the units which are adopted by individual schools will to some extent be influenced by the area in which the school is situated. Let us illustrate this with an example. A school in Colchester, a town with considerable Roman remains, might decide to use this local resource to provide material for a school-designed study unit. The staff might also decide to incorporate evidence uncovered in local archaeological research in the study of 'Domestic Life'. In contrast, a Wiltshire school might prefer to feature a local study unit on 'Wiltshire before the coming of the Romans.'

Programme of Study

Key Stage 1
Pupils should be given opportunities to develop an awareness of the past and of the ways in which it was different from the present. They should be introduced to historical sources of different types.

The programme of study consists of one study unit which should be taught throughout the key stage.

Study Unit
Key elements
Pupils should be helped to develop an awareness of the past through stories from different periods and cultures, including:
- well-known myths and legends;
- stories about historical events;
- eyewitness accounts of historical events;
- fictional stories set in the past.

Pupils should have opportunities to learn about the past from a range of historical sources, including:
- artefacts;
- pictures and photographs;
- music;
- adults talking about their own past;
- written sources;
- buildings and sites;
- computer based materials.

Progressing from familiar situations to those more distant in time and place, pupils should be taught about the everyday life, work, leisure and culture of men, women and children in the past, *for example: clothes, houses, diet, shops, jobs, transport, entertainment.* They should have opportunities to investigate:
- changes in their own lives and those of their family or adults around them;
- changes in the way of life of British people since the Second World War;
- the way of life of people in a period of the past beyond living memory.

Pupils should be taught about the lives of different kinds of famous men and women, *for example: rulers, saints, artists, engineers, explorers, inventors, pioneers.*

Pupils should be taught about past events of different types, including local and national events, events in other countries, and events which have been remembered and commemorated by succeeding generations, *for example: centenaries, religious festivals, anniversaries, the Gunpowder Plot, the Olympic Games.*

Key Stage 2
Pupils should be taught about important episodes and developments in Britain's past, from Roman to modern times. They should have opportunities to investigate local history. They should be taught about ancient civilisations and the history of other parts of the world. They should be helped to develop a sense of chronology and to learn about changes in everyday life over long periods of time.

Pupils should be taught nine study units, selected from, or designed within, the following categories:

Core study units
Either five or six units, which must include:
CSU 1 Invaders and settlers: Romans, Anglo-Saxons, and Vikings in Britain
CSU 2 Tudor and Stuart times

Either or both: CSU 3 Victorian Britain; CSU 4 Britain since 1930
CSU 5 Ancient Greece
CSU 6 Exploration and encounters 1450 to 1550

Supplementary study units
Either three or four units which should complement or extend the core study units . . .

GENERAL REQUIREMENTS

The programme of study should be taught over the four years of the key stage.

Key elements

Pupils should be introduced to the study of history from a variety of perspectives:
• political;
• economic, technological and scientific;
• social;
• religious;
• cultural and aesthetic.

The teaching of the programme of study should involve substantial attention to each perspective across the key stage.

Pupils should be taught about the chronology of the main events and developments in the programme of study.

Pupils should be taught about the social, cultural, religious and ethnic diversity of the societies studied and the experiences of men and women in these societies.

Pupils should have opportunities to learn about the past from a range of historical sources, including:
• documents and printed sources;
• artefacts;
• pictures and photographs;
• music;
• buildings and sites;
• computer based materials.

Supplementary study units
Pupils should be taught **three or four units**, which should include
at least one unit from each of categories A, B and C. Each unit
should make demands comparable to those of a core study unit, in
knowledge, understanding and skills.

**A) A unit involving the study of a theme over a long period of
time**, chosen from:
- Ships and seafarers;
- Food and farming;
- Houses and places of worship;
- Writing and printing;
- Land transport;
- Domestic life, families and childhood.

This unit should:
- involve the study of important historical issues;
- cover a time span of at least 1000 years;
- compare developments in different periods;
- show links between local, British, European and world history.

B) A unit based on local history, which should:
- involve an investigation of an important historical issue;
- relate local developments to national trends;
- involve the study of **one** of the following types of local history:
- — an aspect of the local community over a long period of time, *for
  example: education, leisure, religion*;
- — an aspect of the local community during a short period of time or
  the local community's involvement in a particular event, *for
  example: how the land was enclosed, the First World War*;
- — an aspect of the local community which illustrates developments
  taught in other study units, *for example: Roman settlement,
  child labour in the Industrial Revolution*.

Where two units are taught from this category they should involve
the study of different types of local history.

C) A unit involving the study of a past non-European society,
chosen from:
- Ancient Egypt;
- Mesopotamia;
- Assyria;
- The Indus Valley;
- The Maya;
- Benin.

This unit should:
- involve study from a variety of perspectives: political; economic, technological and scientific; social; religious; cultural and aesthetic;
- introduce pupils to the uses of archaeological evidence;
- cover key features, including the everyday lives of men and women.

Some examples of ways in which the curriculum might be arranged are shown below.

Model A
Greece
Invaders and settlers
Domestic life
A local study
Explorations and encounters
Ships and seafarers
Tudor and Stuart times
Victorian Britain
The Mayan civilisation

Model B
Local study
Ancient Egypt
Invaders and settlers
Land transport through history
Explorations and encounters
Tudor and Stuart times
Life in Britain since 1930
Greece
The Benin civilisation

Model C
Ancient Egypt
Food and farming through
    history
Greece
Invaders and settlers
Local study
Explorations and encounters
Tudor and Stuart times
Victorian Britain
Life in Britain since 1930

Model D
Invaders and settlers
Ships and seafarers through
    history
Tudor and Stuart times
Development of printing and
    writing
Explorations and encounters
Victorian Britain
Life in Britain since 1930
Local study
Ancient civilisations – Assyria

Each model consists of nine units. These nine units have to be taught over a period of four academic years (3–6) and the adoption of a plan of this sort is essential if the curriculum demands are to be met. Once a particular study unit has been chosen the curriculum documentation gives a clear indication of the foci which can profitably be followed within the discipline of four main 'strands' (Political; Economic, technological and scientific; Social and religious; Cultural and aesthetic).

In preparing a study unit, each of these strands will need to be fleshed out and presented in such a way as to give coherence to the study.

Using 'Life in Tudor and Stuart Times' as an example, the unit might be dealt with as follows:

Political

Focus   Court of Henry VIII
          Elizabeth I
          The Armada
          Civil War
          Charles I and Parliament
          Oliver Cromwell

Realised by developing some of the following themes:
The 'new' monarchy – Henry VII
Tudor and Stuart monarchs
Trial and execution of Charles I
Cromwell in Ireland
The settlements in the New World
Plots and rebellions
People: Lord Burley; William Cecil; Thomas More; Cardinal Wolsey

Social and Religious

Focus   Life style of different social groups and religious sects
          Great Plague 1665
          Great Fire of London 1666
          Religious conflict and persecution
          Wales in Tudor times

Realised by developing some of the following themes:
The family in Tudor times
The family in Cromwellian times
The family in early/late Stuart times
Being poor, being rich, being young
Courtship and marriage
Costume and fashion
Houses and hovels
Furniture, fittings, decoration
Eating, drinking, cooking, preserving
Foods from abroad
Witchcraft, magic and superstition
Life in the city (eg London, York, Chester)
Life in the countryside
Sports and games
The Pilgrim Fathers
Martyrs – Catholic and Protestant
The King James Bible
People, eg John Aubrey; Archbishop Cranmer; John Bunyan; John Evelyn; Inigo Jones; Mary, Queen of Scots; Samuel Pepys; Robert Smythson (architect); John Stowe (diarist); John Thynne (architect); Christopher Wren

Economic, technical and scientific

Focus Agriculture
Towns, trade and transport
Exploration
Scientific discovery

Realised by developing some of the following themes:
Drake's voyages 1577–1580
Search for the NW Passage
Search for the NE Passage (Willoughby)
Settlements in the New World
Ships, cargoes and their destinations
Coinage, prices, wages
Clocks, sundials, telescopes
Alchemy and astronomy
Travel on land
Raising animals and poultry
Growing food – vegetables, fruits, herbs
Industry – the development of fabrics
Mines and mining, coal and iron
Building materials, building methods
Machines and power – wind, water, animal
Maps and map makers
Shops, fairs and markets
People, eg Francis Bacon; William Harvey (physician); Isaac
Newton; John Tradescant (botonist)

Cultural and aesthetic

Focus Architecture
Music and Drama

Realised by developing some of the following themes:
The Tudor palace
The Jacobean mansion
The Yeoman's house
Tudor houses in Tudor times
The use of brick, timber frame, stone
Theatres in Tudor and Stuart times
Masques, progresses and entertainments
Fairs
Dance and dancing
Writing and printing
Life in Oxford and Cambridge
People eg:

- Artists: Nicholas Hilliard; Hans Holbein; Van Dyck
- Musicians: William Byrd; John Dowland; Richard Farrant; Thomas Morely; Thomas Tallis
- Playwrights and actors: Edward Alleyn; Richard Burbage; Ben Jonson; William Shakespeare
- Writers and poets: Francis Beaumont, John Donne; John Dryden; John Fletcher; George Herbert; Christopher Marlowe; Andrew Marvell; John Milton; Edmund Spencer.

From such a framework, particular aspects can be developed and emphasised by drawing upon materials held in school (eg books, tapes, discs) and by using local resources (a Stuart building, Tudor artefacts displayed in a nearby museum etc). Thus a visit to a house built in 1623 would allow for an analysis of building materials (walls, floors, ceilings, roofs, doors, windows); decoration (on wood, stone, brick, plaster); the use of the rooms (house design) facilities for cooking and sanitation (including water supply). If appropriate, furniture, paintings and floor and wall coverings could also be studied.

The school-designed history units can be analysed in a similar fashion. If, for example, the focus is to be upon a study of the development of the village, ways in which the study embraces the three targets:

- Knowledge and understanding of history
- Interpretation of history
- Use of historical sources

are illuminated through the four component strands. Thus a village study might range over the following:

Political
Focus Significant events in the history of our village which have influenced its development
    a) the impact of central government
    b) the impact of local landowners
    c) the impact of local organisations
    d) the impact of events outside its immediate area

Realised by developing some of the following themes:
Settlement – from early times to the present day
The Roman road
The Saxon church (remains)
The Norman motte
The new church (1190)
The Elizabethan manor
Fields – enclosures, the manor house

The Toll house
The Workhouse
The Village Memorial Hall (1918)
The Festival of Britain award
The New Estate (1987)
Parish and Vestry records
Census returns
The stocks

Economic, technological, scientific
Focus   Agriculture
          Machines and Tools
          Communication
          Industry (if any)

Realised by developing some of the following themes:
Early and contemporary maps
Building styles and materials (cf the church and the modern estate)
Local building methods – using flint and brick
The millstream
The agricultural machine repair workshop
Agriculture – tools and equipment, changes over the past 200 years
The battery hen units
New crops – rape
The village pump
The smithy (derelict)
The village shop and its services
Public transport
Tourism, B & B, farm holidays

Social and religious
Focus   The coming of Christianity
          New sects

Realised by developing some of the following themes:
The parish church through history
The parish graveyard
The Wesleyan chapel
The (C of E) Primary School
Changes in the life of ordinary people as illustrated by buildings
Oral history – local people's memories of the past, present occupations
The village in postcard, print, guidebook, county history
War memorials – South African; Great War; Second World War
Village associations and clubs
Church celebrations and festivals eg Rogationtide, Christmas, Harvest

Cultural and aesthetic
Focus Arts and crafts

Realised by developing some of the following themes:
Local crafts – reed thatching
Decoration and pattern in local building
Doom painting in church
Carvings on bench ends
The morris dancers
Local customs eg Well dressing
Local craftsmen and women who use modern technology eg the glass
engraver, the furniture maker
The village school
The local pub
Villagers today, their pastimes and organisations.

The significance of the individual elements within the lists above
will need to be carefully examined before a study unit is finally
devised. So will the teaching strategies which will be required to
explore it. Often the local study, because it uses familiar themes,
facilitates understanding. The glass engraver now working in an
outhouse once used by the village blacksmith gives immediate
insight into change over time; the use of wood in the stocks, in gates
and stiles, and as framework for houses and the windmill indicates
how dependent our ancestors were upon the skills of the master
carpenter (as well as upon a plentiful supply of seasoned wood).

A locally focused study unit will uncover a wide range of material,
not all of it immediately usable. Nevertheless *all* of the material
should be saved. Children in Year 3 are likely to demand less
detailed information than those in Year 6. However, 'surplus'
material may well be needed at some later date, perhaps when units
in the history programme are being re-arranged following curriculum re-organisation.

References

1   *History for ages 5 to 16* Proposals of the Secretary of State for
    Education & Science. D.E.S. London, July 1990 and the response
    of The National Curriculum Council. December 1990.

8 Assessing the programme

Now what I want is facts. Teach these boys and girls nothing but facts

Charles Dickens *Hard Times* Chapter 1

We need to establish a curriculum which has no subject barriers, a curriculum beyond the preconditioned, fed by a range of inputs – pedagogic, social, cultural.

Pietro Prini, the Italian philosopher addressing the UNESCO conference on Heritage Education, Paris, November 1989.

It follows, since Standard Assessment Tasks (SATS) are not to be applied to History at Key Stages 1 and 2, that the non-statutory assessment tasks may therefore be used by teachers 'as and when they judge fit' (DES spokesperson). Since assessments made by teachers within each school will provide the basis for establishing what pupils have achieved at the end of each Key Stage, it follows that methods of recording will reflect the individuality of teachers and of the schools in which they work.

It has been said that the art of teaching implies a conscious intention to help others acquire knowledge, concepts, ideas and skills or, put another way, that learning is the acquisition by the learner of that body of knowledge and concepts, ideas and skills which are central to any academic study. The teacher, working alone in a classroom with 30 eight-year-olds, may agree intellectually with such a definition. The task of fulfilling its demands in every curriculum area is daunting and extremely difficult to achieve. The problem is not simply one of classroom organisation and management. The individuality of each child (learner) has to be taken into account. As Her Majesty's Inspectors observe: 'It must be recognised that there is no one standard which is appropriate to all children at a given age'.[1]

That said, the task remains. As teachers we are responsible for ensuring that learning happens, that the classroom environment exposes growing minds to knowledge in its many varied forms.

Assessment (of teacher and of child) is a way of establishing the degree of effectiveness of teaching and of learning. In the field of history how might this be achieved?

Assessment of children's progress will take many forms. In years 1 and 2 it is likely to be informal and to reflect the individual enthusiasms and responses (written, oral, pictorial) of the children who make up the class. Thus the teacher's assessments will undoubtedly be descriptive, history being but one of many elements which will be touched upon in the final overall report (end of Key Stage 1).

As children move through years 3 to 6 a rather more precise analysis is both needful and appropriate. By the age of 11, with increasing ability to read and to write, children should show facility to research information, to set their studies within a basic chronology and terminology and to be aware of the particular elements (concepts and skills) which are central to history.

In this respect the following checklist might prove useful for it provides a framework within which we can assess each child within the class.

Assessment checklist

Historical element	*Indicator of individual understanding*
Chronology	Has an awareness of historical terms eg BC, AD, decade, generation, century, epoch. Is able to sequence dates and periods. Is able to sequence artefacts (including buildings) and pictures. Is able to relate events to a time chart
Evidence	Is able to understand the kind of evidence which is used by the historian. Is able to distinguish between primary and secondary evidence. Is aware of the need to be critical when assessing evidence. Has some awareness of how historians use evidence to reach an explanation of an event in the past.

Language	Has understanding of words used within an historic context. Included in the History Study Units, Key Stage 2, Units 2–12, are: *Aristocracy, Authority, Civil War, Class, Conquest, Conversion, Custom, Democracy, Depression, Emigration, Empire, Evacuation, Exploration, Government, Immigration, Industry, Inheritance, Invasion, Law, Manorial, Monarch, Myth, Parliament, Religious, Settlement, Trade, Yeoman.*
Similarity, difference	Is able to make simple comparison between past and present against a range of different periods and different cultures and contrasting social contexts.
Continuity, change	Has an awareness and understanding that history is both a study of continuity and a study of change. Is able to understand that an event in history may have many contributory causes.
Empathy	Is able to relate sympathetically to people who were alive in the past whose views, attitudes, culture and time perspective differ from his/her own.

Such a checklist can serve as a guide to the aspects of history teaching which have been neglected. However it will not indicate the effectiveness of learning and teaching.

Some schools may decide to set tests to establish levels of understanding. However current practice (concept and skill-based learning) places much less emphasis on facts learned parrot-fashion and so makes traditional methods of testing difficult to implement.

A more effective, though more demanding, method of assessment is for each child to keep examples of his/her history in a loose leaf folder (a folded sheet of A2 is ideal). Into this, at regular intervals through years 3 to 6, is placed an example of history studies . . . a picture, an account of a visit, a piece of imaginative writing, a description of an historical event and so on. Each sheet is dated. It is this material which will eventually be used as the basis for Key Stage assessment for such records will clearly show each child's individual development.*

Into each file, at the end of each academic year and on a change of teacher, a sheet is inserted listing the topics covered by the class. (Only one A4 sheet will be prepared and photocopied. Thus an identical sheet will accompany each child's folder, the contents only being amended in respect of children who have joined the class mid-year.) This teacher's record sheet will prove useful to colleagues who receive children in subsequent academic years (ie movement of children between teachers in the same school in years 3–6) and between schools (the file being transferred with other school records).

The method described above was employed for the principal curriculum areas in the school of which I was headteacher. The files were kept centrally. They proved an efficient and reliable method of monitoring progress over both long and short term. It was not unduly time consuming – indeed less so than detailed written teacher records. When they left primary school, every child mounted their personal 'Primary Record' into a large scrapbook. This was taken home and often used at the initial meetings of the children and their parents with the teachers who were to be responsible for them at secondary school.

In order to better appreciate how such material can be used let us examine some examples of children's written work.

Hampton Court, by Manny, aged 7

It was built in 1514 for Thomas Wolsey and King Henry the VIII got jealous and angry so he gave it to him to make him happy. When Thomas Wolsey had it he had 500 servants. But Henry was not happy.

Then we went back to school. We got the number 4 bus to get to school and we got the train to get the bus.

Here we have the blur of time past and time present, typical of many children of this age. Nevertheless the piece suggests an awareness of then and now and that historical figures had feelings and sometimes behaved rather like us.

---

* Work placed in the folder can consist of final copies of preliminary drafts – a process recommended in 'English in the National Curriculum'.[2]

Manny's writing (which was accompanied with a picture) was produced at the same time as that of Aidan.

A visit to Hampton Court, by Aidan aged 7

Hampton Court was built by Thomas Wolsey first. Then Henry VIII bought it because Thomas wanted to get favour with Henry. Henry made new wings on it. Now it has 1004 rooms. In Clock Court we found a white building which was the way into the State apartments. We went through lots of rooms (listed). We went to the haunted gallery where Ann Boleyn's screamy ghost can still be heard. In the Great Hall and the Royal Chapel the King was raised up while the people sat below.

We saw a vine that was planted in 1768. One flower bed does not have any plants in it cause the roots of the vine are under it. We saw sunken gardens. After that we went back to the station.

Here we have an example of the fluency of a competent seven-year-old. In assessing a piece of work of this quality it is apparent that the visit triggered a range of responses ... history through events (the screamy ghost), history through evidence (the old vine), history as people (Wolsey, Henry, Ann), history as landscape (the gardens), history as change (the new wings), history as custom (the Royal Chapel).

Archaeologist, by Kate aged 8

We went to East Tenter Street where some builders were about to build a block of flats. We met the archaeologist who had found a Roman burial ground underneath the rubbish. We learned how they dug up bones and pottery and, at their base we saw how they washed and dried the objects. We saw part of a Roman bow.

It was strange to think of a burial ground near a modern office block.

In this piece Kate indicates that she is developing a sense of historical time and is beginning to experiment with classification (such as 'Roman'). A subsequent piece of work made it apparent that she was not yet able to relate 'Roman' to 'Norman'. Nevertheless Kate does show an awareness of now (the rebuilding) and the past (the burial ground).

The Cruck House, by Ann, aged 8

We saw a very old cruck house. A cruck house is made with oak beams like this. Two beams are put upwards making an arch. Then a long pole is put on the top and two other poles are put on each side. There can be as many arches as you like. On top of the three poles there are rafters, on top of the rafters, thatch. One end of the cruck house is for the people, the other end is for the animals. The cruck house I saw had a salt box in the fireplace. Salt was precious so the King put a tax on it and to keep the salt dry people would put a salt box near the fire. The person sitting nearest the salt is the most important person. The cruck house had a witch post to keep evil spirits away.

Ann was a very able child and was able to write an accurate account of the house she visited (part of a study of homes and housing). The building was situated in an open museum and Ann was confident enough to be able to describe it and to add numerous incidental details (salt, the witch post).

Being poor in Victorian Times by Sarah, aged 8

Two men are walking down the street.
They pass me and ignore me.
They know I'm there.
They whisper; I'm scared.
They pass me again and stop.
I'm shivering and starved.
Why do they ignore me, I do not know?
They walk round the corner, will they come back?
I do not know if I want them back.
They are not cruel or are they?
No one knows, only them.
I'm dirty; everyone is dirty around here, it's true.
There has got to be another explanation.
But what?
I give up.
I'm walking down the street,
curious, will I meet them again?

This piece of writing followed upon some work on Victorian London and an urban trail to look for examples of Victorian buildings which are still to be seen. There is an indication within the poem of the historical dimension in which it is rooted – yet it gives a strong feeling of a time other than now.

'Flatford Mill' by Susan, aged 9

Then the grass grew by the side of the river.
Now there is nothing but a muddy path
With trees overhanging.
Then there were barges in the clear blue water.
Now there are no barges
And the water is muddy.
Then the lock gates moved smoothly,
Now they are rusty with lack of use.
Then the cottages were white and bright,
With men and boys playing outside.
Now they are grey and still.
But the river still goes on
Through years and years
While people come
And people go.

This poem indicates a very strong sense of continuity and change. This awareness is reflected in the linking of the river (unchanging) to the people who have lived alongside it and their work.

Appeal by Mark, aged 10

Winchester
Christmas 873

Your Majesty

Greetings. I write to you for help. The bad winter and fear of the Danes has caused some of our lay brothers to flee the monastery. We who stay here are finding it hard to survive and do the things asked of us. The roof of the nave needs repairing and our writings are unfinished. Can you send us food. The Peace of Christ be with you.

Brother Mark

Mark's writing shows that he understands something of the problems of the monks of Winchester, the difficulties of living at a time of war and the people's dependence upon the King for protection. It indicates sympathy for the plight of the monk and records the type of work which a monk might have had to undertake.

Bartholomew Fair by Robert, aged 10

This fair was first held in 1133, on Smoothefield, or Smithfield. It was where Rahere, Henry I's jester, got enough money to build a church and a hospital. He got the money from collecting the toll from the fair.

The church and the hospital are still there. The fair lasted over 700 years. At first it was really a place to buy goods, but some people thought the buyers might like some entertainment as well, so they set up small stalls around the edge of the fair. These soon took over the goods stalls.

At the fair there was even a court with a special judge for people who committed a crime there. This was called the Court of Pie Powder, which means 'dusty feet' (Pieds poudres) in French because fair people were travellers.

The entertainments were very different then. There were Morris dancers, jugglers, clowns and tumblers, dancing bears, puppet shows. There were stalls selling greasy pork and ginger-bread saints. There were freaks and monsters to look at – bearded ladies, a mermaid, and the fattest woman in the world. Everybody would be shouting out what was for sale.

This piece of writing explores continuity and change, and clearly acknowledges that people in the past had a lifestyle which was peculiar and particular to them. The writing is descriptive, not judgemental. It was rooted in a re-enactment of the Fair which had been researched at the London Museum, St Bartholomews, Smithfield and through studying some extracts of Ben Jonson's play.

My school, by Joanne aged 11

In 1870 Parliament passed an Education Act stating that all children between 5–12 had to attend school. Until then only those whose parents could afford the cost of up to sixpence a week (2.5p) had any education: Board schools like our school were built all over London. Our foundation stone is dated 1891 but the school was opened on 27 February 1893. It had been built at a cost of £18,959 when the average terraced house cost £150–£200. By 1904 there were 1,634 pupils on roll.

Joanne's writing indicates an ability to compare and contrast, to incorporate simple statistics into her report and to draw attention to the unusual facts she had discovered (eg the two dates).

Bosworth, 1485, by Timothy, aged 11

Timothy's interest in Richard III was fired by a visit to the National Portrait Gallery. On returning to school he found a map which showed the Battle. He copied it, but noticed that it had been drawn onto a contemporary map which showed modern roads (see Figure 8.1).

He then decided to try to draw the battle from the map he had found 'as though it was then' (Figure 8.2).

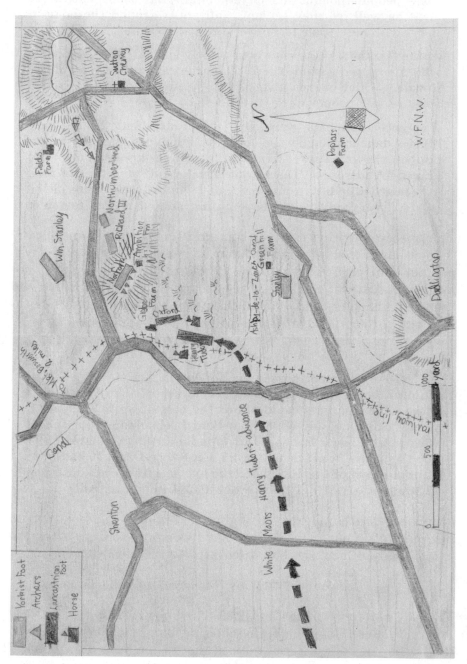

Figure 8.1

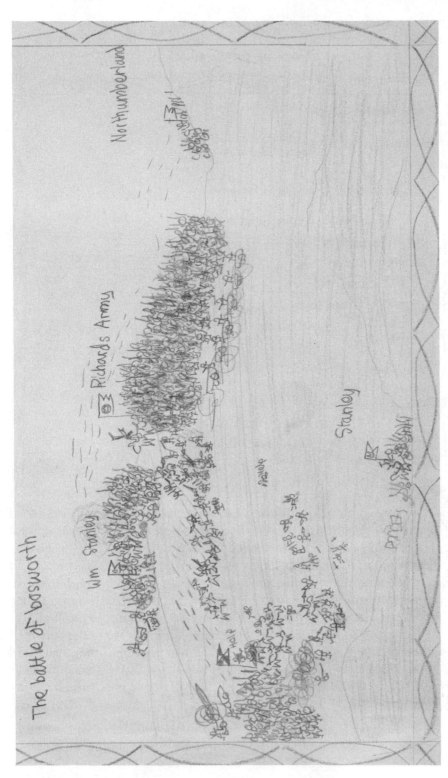

Figure 8.2

So interested did he become that he tried to find reasons why Richard might not have killed the Princes. Figures 8.3 and 8.4 are two of the evidence sheets he produced.

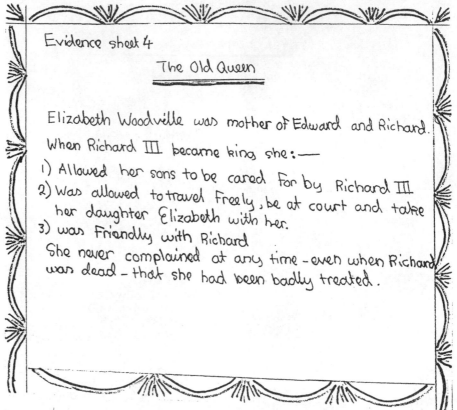

Evidence sheet 4

The Old Queen

Elizabeth Woodville was mother of Edward and Richard.

When Richard III became king she:—

1) Allowed her sons to be cared for by Richard III
2) Was allowed to travel freely, be at court and take her daughter Elizabeth with her.
3) was friendly with Richard

She never complained at any time - even when Richard was dead - that she had been badly treated.

Figure 8.3

In all of these examples children have expressed ideas and presented information. Each fulfils, at an appropriate level, an individual child's response to an historical topic. While these writings may be set and evaluated against the given attainment targets in history, it should be remembered that they may also be used for assessment in other curriculum areas: Ann's writing on the construction of a house provides an interesting comment on medieval technology; Joanne's draws upon a range of statistical sources; Timothy is concerned with the presentation of a sequence of events through language and pictures; Susan and Sarah write in blank verse; Kate's account is in simple prose, while Aidan and Mark allow themselves to marry fact and imagination.

I would suggest that these examples demonstrate that one piece of work can indicate understanding across Key Stages and attainment levels. We are far better able to judge a child's achievement from the

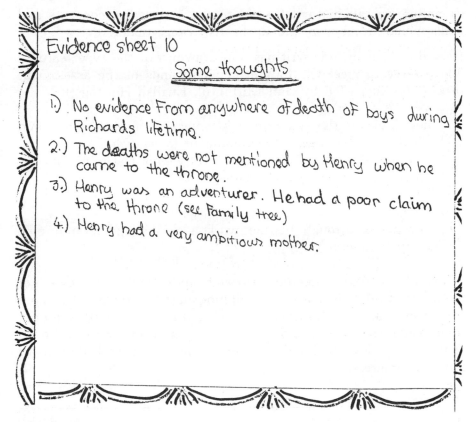

Evidence sheet 10

Some thoughts

1.) No evidence from anywhere of death of boys during Richards lifetime.

2.) The deaths were not mentioned by Henry when he came to the throne.

3.) Henry was an adventurer. He had a poor claim to the throne (see family tree)

4.) Henry had a very ambitious mother.

Figure 8.4

examination of a range of writings than from a set test (however sympathetically administered). One piece of work may indicate that a child is beginning to be able to set his/her work against the framework of chronological time, a second piece, written some months later, may indicate an awareness of the need to refer to evidence. An observation: 'Do you see! On this 1380 map there are no railway lines and no big roads' (nine-year-old) made in discussion may suggest a certain sympathetic understanding of a person long dead or a drawing point to the ability to research with accuracy.

If we accept that the ways of assessing children's progress are many and varied and that it is almost impossible to determine with accuracy that 'every child has made the learning their own', assessment will very much depend upon 'teacher awareness'. 'Although little in the way of formal assessment was undertaken, the teachers were aware of the quality of work produced'[3]. All that assessment should seek to do is to provide information about children's understanding, knowledge and progress in the academic discipline we call history, 'linked to the knowledge, concepts and skills which are appropriate to the Key Stage under review.'[4]

Records which include writings and drawings of the type featured above serve to meet the four principal strands of the assessment process (as suggested by Gail Durbin of 'English Heritage'):

1   They indicate the positive achievements of each pupil and indicate possible areas of development (*formative*).
2   They indicate areas of learning difficulty – not just in history but in presentation/recording etc (*diagnostic*).
3   They indicate overall achievement in a systematic way (*summative*).
4   They assess through his/her work a child's understanding of history (*evaluative*).

Longitudinal record keeping through individual anthologies of children's work has two other significant advantages over more prescribed methods. It provides teacher and parent with material upon which to make considered judgements. More important even than this, it allows each child to monitor and to be critical of his or her own progress.

Teacher's checklist

Preparation

1   What specific area of historical study do I plan to undertake?
2   How does this study relate to the History Study Units and the attainment targets (and the knowledge, skills and concepts) to which they relate?
3   How will I a) introduce, b) develop the activities and ensure that they link with other curriculum areas and objectives?
4   How will I find out what the children already know about the topic they are to study?
5   What will I need to prepare before introducing the topic to the class (eg books, photocopied materials, pictures, audio-visual aids, visits)?
6   What gaps will I have to fill in my own knowledge?
7   Will the study challenge the most able children in my class?
8   Am I to involve other teaching staff in the programme? What will be their role?

9   Am I to involve other adults in the activity (eg parents, museum staff, local people)? What preparation will they need?

Delivery

1   What kinds of activities will the children undertake? Are there specific areas of concept/skill development upon which these activities will focus?

2   How will these activities help meet objectives in other curriculum areas, eg analytic, descriptive and creative writing, note taking, discussions, the interpretation of data in charts and diagrams, the use of a simple database?

3   How will the activities be organised within the classroom? What demands will be made upon particular children (eg those with special needs, bilingual children, gifted children)?

4   What range of outcomes are envisaged:
   • spoken
   • written (in what forms?)
   • pictures and models in a range of media (see Figures 8.5–8.8)
   • displays (group and class; museum table; artefacts; documents)
   • dance and music
   • presentation at a school assembly?

5   How will the children's individual achievements be recorded
   • by the teacher?
   • by the child (eg in an ongoing history folder which follows each child through his/her primary years)?

6   How will the findings be shared across the class?

Review and evaluation

1   How successful was the approach which was followed?

2   Did it encourage the children to develop enquiry techniques in their learning of history?

3   What criteria were used to arrive at this conclusion?

4   Did the activity result in progression (ie sophisticated tasks undertaken more successfully than before)?

5   Was the study appropriate to the age, aptitude and abilities of the children taking part?

6   Were the questions asked of the children sufficiently demanding? Using the classifications-model devised by Gail Durbin of 'English Heritage', were children asked

Figure 8.5 *Ways of recording – through drawing, a ten-year-old's impression of Chichester Cathedral.*

Figure 8.6 — *through photography, an eight-year-old's photograph at Pickering, N. Yorks.*

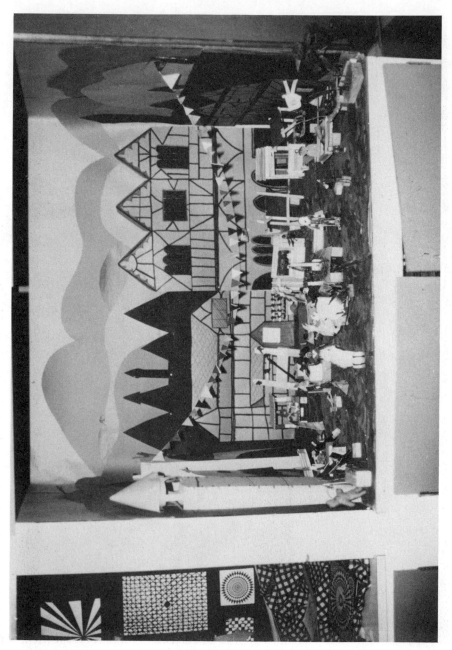

Figure 8.7 – *through model making, a Medieval market (nine-year-olds).*

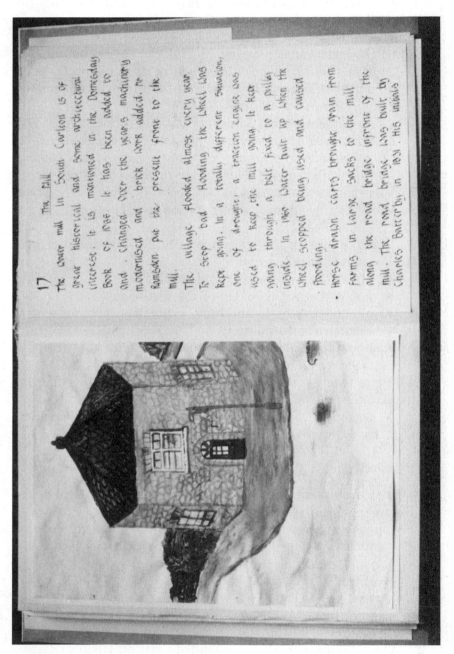

Figure 8.8 – *through words and pictures, ten-year-olds. (Reproduced by kind permission of the Civic Trust)*

- Memory questions (eg *What year was it when . . .?*)
- Convergent questions (eg *In what way is this tool like this one? How do you think this piece of equipment worked?*)
- Divergent questions (eg *imagine you are trying to escape from this priest hole? How many different routes could you plan, bearing in mind that the garden is surrounded by Roundhead soldiers?*)
- Judgemental questions (eg *Do you think it right that Bristol sea captains traded in slaves? What does this tell us about their attitudes to the men, women and children their ships carried from Africa to the Americas?*)

7   Were the lessons varied in pace, content, tone, ethos, style?
8   Did the study address, where appropriate, cross-cultural and gender issues?
9   Was the pace of the study too fast/too slow/about right?
10   What has been learned:
- about the historical period studied;
- about the methodology of the historian;
- about ways of researching, evaluating and presenting historical information;
- about individual children, their particular gifts, insights, strengths and weaknesses?

11   Were the tasks set always clearly identified and differentiated?
12   What evidence was there that the children were keen and actively involved in their history work?

Reflections for the future ('a curriculum audit')

1   As a consequence of undertaking this study, what particular elements can be identified as:
- positive and supportive, eg library or museum resource, involvement of local people and institutions, audio and visual materials held in school or in a local resource centre?
- negative, eg in what way could the study have been better introduced and planned; could it have been better resourced?

2   What elements might be extended/omitted when undertaking a similar activity in the future?

Action

1 With whom on the school staff should observations/reflections be shared:
   • the head or deputy?
   • the teacher responsible for curriculum development?
2 Do any of the observations merit inclusion in 'whole school' policy?

References

1 *Primary Education in England* A Report by Her Majesty's Inspectors of Schools HMSO London, 1978.
2 *English in the National Curriculum* HMSO London, 1989
3 & 4   *The Teaching and Learning of History and Geography* HMSO London, 1989

9 A personal framework

'A child is not a vase to be filled but a fire to be kindled'
Francois Rabelais

The earlier chapters of this book examined the place and purpose of introducing young children to the academic study we call history. As we have seen, to enter this study children will need a range of skills. They will need, for example, to be shown how to question evidence, to be sceptical; to be helped to understand the nature of change within continuity and the nature of cause; to develop a sense of chronology; to be helped to empathise with people whose motives, expectations and aspirations are perhaps alien from their own. This skill- and concept-based approach to the teaching of history may be used to focus upon any period of history and upon any culture. It is as appropriate to the historical study of a subcontinent (like India) or a nation state, the history of a tiny village, an individual house, a family or the inhabitants of a town.

Thus an understanding of history which depends upon each child making such concepts his/her own and mastering the skills (reading, relating, recording) necessary to discover and unravel the material to hand, has much to commend it. Such an approach need not rely upon an imposed temporal framework; we can teach the methodology of the historian by taking children into any detailed study of time past (whether this be the time of the Egyptian Pharaoh or of the Firewatcher on the Home Front).

In recent years those responsible for the curriculum of our schools (politicians, the national and local inspectorate, teacher trainers, heads and teachers) have been consumed with the production of models, a multitude of structures which, when bolted in place, will help ensure that learning is effective. We who value history may draw some comfort from the fact that it has been included in this exercise and that it merits some space within the national model. As a consequence of this recognition, history will occupy (in some cases for the first time) an assured place on the timetable of every state school.

And yet, in welcoming this advance, great care must be taken not to allow textbook-led activities to become the focus of classroom work. If history teaching is to be successful, the learners' intelligence must be quickened, the imagination awakened. This desired end is unlikely to be achieved by the force feeding of pre-determined facts, supported by work which has no personal dimension. In this respect the coming of the core curriculum makes the teacher's role even more important. Young people need to question their nation's past, be able to reflect upon heritage, have security in knowing their own roots. To do this effectively they will need to be taught an appropriate methodology and given the skills necessary to apply it.

To a large extent our preoccupation with a national, local or school-based framework is misconceived. In the long term the historical framework which matters is that which each child creates within him or herself. We know from research[1] that children acquire much of their historical information from sources outside school (TV, visits with parents to places of interest, films, stories, even comics and children's newspapers). Jahoda's findings (see page 23) suggest that children move towards an understanding of historical time in a personal, pragmatic way.

The temporal framework which they construct *is their own* and may bear little relationship to the temporal framework imposed by either school text or curriculum designer. Hopefully the variety of approaches which children will meet during their early years of schooling and the variety of topics which are covered will help them to achieve it, for the creation of such a framework implies the heightening of historical awareness within each child.

A dilemma remains. History, a study of men and women in the past, is so vast a tapestry that it is difficult to know where the first tentative entry should be made in order to provide a starting point from which a 'personal framework' can develop. The 'core' approach provides an answer, but the concentration upon a 'core' can so easily stifle personal development and force the teacher to present the past in packaged units – and so set the flow of history in stone.

It is here that theory and practice conflict. Intellectually and theoretically it seems appropriate to equip all of a nation's children with a body of knowledge (or facts) and the skills necessary to interpret them. Such an observation could apply to every academic discipline. However, in attempting to tease out the essential factual elements of such a framework for the study of history it is almost impossible to jettison national and personal prejudices. For example it could be that an agreed centralised framework carries covert messages about national pride (eg heroes and heroines of the British Empire), common identity (eg the holocaust as a central element of Israeli history), or hint at injustice (eg the colonisation of the

Malvinas to children in schools in Argentina). Thus it may be that temporal frameworks which are imposed are likely to confirm how a nation sees itself and that the materials made available to teachers (whether the curriculum be locally or nationally established) will reflect this perception.

We should seek, therefore, to avoid presenting history in terms of an unfleshed skeleton of the past. Of course a series of dates which pinpoint certain historical events could be used to take children through the nation's history. But these events, arbitrarily selected, are unlikely to provide the starting point from which young people will eventually be able to move towards a critical understanding of any happening in their nation's past – be the happening the passage of a Bill of Rights, a massacre at York or the writings of Adam Smith.

Reflecting upon their own fact-filled school days will surely encourage contemporary educationalists to question the value of rote learning of facts which are unrelated to children's needs or experience. The chanting of tables to enable pupils to spit out an immediate response to the question 'What is 7×12?' when imperial measures were in common use could be seen by the learner (as he or she struggled with pence and shillings) to have some practical application. A child's ability to comment upon the years 55 BC, 410, 1066, 1389, 1662, 1776, 1834 or 1911 is much more difficult to justify, either in terms of practical need, or in terms of knowledge worth retaining.

As Jean Barthelemy observed in a paper presented at the 1st UNESCO Colloque on Heritage Education (Paris, 1989), the 'doors of our schools must open'. Only when they do can teacher and taught begin to acknowledge their common heritage 'through history, culture and landscape'.

Whatever the pressures of curriculum implementation I remain hopeful that such a dream will be realised.

References

1   West, John 'Young children's awareness of the past' *Trends in Education*, Spring Issue, 1978

Appendix   The National Curriculum

RECOMMENDATIONS FOR ATTAINMENT TARGETS AND STATE-
MENTS OF ATTAINMENT
(from National Curriculum Council *History in the National Curriculum*,
March 1991)

*The examples printed in italics serve to illustrate the statements of
attainment and are non-statutory.*

Attainment target 1: Knowledge and understanding of history

The development of the ability to describe and explain historical change
and cause, and analyse different features of historical situations.

LEVEL		STATEMENTS OF ATTAINMENT	EXAMPLES
		Demonstrating their knowledge of the historical context in the programmes of study, pupils should be able to:	
1.	a)	place in sequence events in a story about the past.	*Re-tell the story of the Gunpowder Plot.*
	b)	give reasons for their own actions.	*Explain why they chose to take part in an activity.*
2.	a)	place familiar objects in chronological order.	*Put a series of personal and family photographs and belongings in chronological order.*
	b)	explain why people in the past acted as they did.	*Explain why Boudicca fought against the Romans.*
	c)	identify differences between past and present.	*Talk about how life in a Viking village differed from life today.*
3.	a)	describe changes over a period of time.	*Make a wall display showing changes in the way of life of the last two generations.*
	b)	give a reason for an historical event or development.	*Select from a list of possible causes one reason why in Victorian times railways became a more important form of transport than canals.*
	c)	identify differences between times in the past.	*Talk about differences between an ancient Greek temple and a medieval cathedral.*
4.	a)	recognise that over time some things changed and others stayed the same.	*Identify aspects of everyday life which have changed greatly over the last hundred years and others which have changed very little.*

LEVEL	STATEMENTS OF ATTAINMENT	EXAMPLES
	b) show an awareness that historical events usually have more than one cause and consequence.	*Suggest more than one cause and consequence of the Black Death.*
	c) describe different features of an historical period.	*Arrange, label and display pictures, maps and diagrams which illustrate aspects of life in Tudor Britain.*
5.	a) distinguish between different kinds of historical change.	*Group some of the changes in nineteenth century Britain under the headings 'rapid' or 'gradual' and 'local' or 'national'.*
	b) identify different types of cause and consequence.	*Suggest some political and social causes and consequences, short-term and long-term, of the fall of the Roman Empire.*
	c) show how different features in an historical situation relate to each other.	*Write an account of Drake's voyage around the world, linking different aspects (for example: political, economic, scientific, etc.)*

Attainment target 2: Interpretations of history

The development of the ability to understand interpretations of history.

LEVEL	STATEMENTS OF ATTAINMENT	EXAMPLES
	Demonstrating their knowledge of the historical content in the programmes of study, pupils should be able to:	
1.	understand that stories may be about real people or fictional characters.	*Recognise the difference between a fairytale and a story about the past.*
2.	show an awareness that different stories about the past can give different versions of what happened.	*Detect differences in two adults' accounts of the same past event.*
3.	distinguish between a fact and a point of view.	*Recognise that the statement 'Alfred was King of Wessex' is a fact, and that the statement 'King Alfred was a good man' is a point of view.*
4.	show an understanding that deficiencies in evidence may lead to different interpretations of the past.	*Show how lack of evidence about ancient Egypt might be one reason why pictures in different books portray Egyptian life in different ways.*

LEVEL	STATEMENTS OF ATTAINMENT	EXAMPLES
5.	recognise that interpretations of the past, including popular accounts, may differ from what is known to have happened.	*Show in discussion an understanding that Magna Carta is often mistakenly remembered as a charter which laid down the rights of ordinary people.*

Attainment target 3: The use of historical sources

The development of pupils' ability to acquire evidence from historical sources, and form judgements about their reliability and value.

LEVEL	STATEMENTS OF ATTAINMENT	EXAMPLES
	Demonstrating their knowledge of the historical content in the programmes of study, pupils should be able to:	
1.	communicate information acquired from an historical source.	*Talk about what they see in an old photograph.*
2.	recognise that historical sources can stimulate and help answer questions about the past.	*Show how artefacts in a museum can help answer the question 'how did people cook before they had gas or electricity'?*
3.	make deductions from historical sources.	*Make simple deductions about social groups in Victorian Britain by looking at the clothes people wore.*
4.	put together information drawn from different historical sources.	*Use information from old newspapers, photographs and maps to descripe a local street in the 1930s.*
5.	comment on the usefulness of an historical source by reference to its content, as evidence for a particular enquiry.	*Talk about how information gained from a visit to an old house can be used to reconstruct the way of life of its former inhabitants.*

Note

As with other National Curriculum programmes the targets relate to 10 distinct levels of attainment. Bearing in mind that these levels relate to *individual* children, the range of attainment within any one class or age group is likely to be considerable. Thus the report recommends that the attainment of children at Key Stage 1 will range between levels 1–3 and at Key Stage 2 between levels 2–5.

Bibliography

Architecture and Landscape
Adams, E and Ward, C (1982) *Art and the Built Environment*, Longman, London.

Braun, H (1951) *Introduction to English Medieval Architecture*, Faber, London.

Hoskins, W G (1979) *Reading the Landscape*, BBC Publications, London.

Muir, Richard (1981) *Reading the Landscape*, Michael Joseph, London.

Neal, P (1987) *The Urban Scene, Considering Conservation*, Dryad Press, Leicester.

Whittock, R (1987) *Explaining Buildings*, Wayland, London.

Customs
Hartley, D (1979) *The Land of England*, Macdonald, London.

Defence
Brown, Allen, R (1976 edn) *English Castles*, Batsford, London.

Johnston, Forde (1979) *Great Medieval Castles of Britain*, Guilding Publishing (BCA), London.

Simpson, Douglas (1969) *Castles in England and Wales*, Batsford, London.

Ecclesiastical
Anderson, M D (1971) *History and Imagery in English Churches*, John Murray, London.

Braun, H (1970) *Parish Churches*, Faber, London.

Braun, H (1971) *English Abbeys*, Faber, London.

Foster, R (1981) *Discovering English Churches*, BBC, London.

Hogg, Gary (1972) *Priories and Abbeys of England*, David & Charles, Newton Abbot.

Jones, Lawrence (1978) *The Beauty of English Churches*, Constable, London.

Smith, E et al (1976) *English Parish Churches*, Thames and Hudson, London.

Watkins, P and Hughes, E (1980) *Here's the Church*, Julia MacRae, London.

Industrial
Bailey, B (1972) *Industrial Heritage of Britain*, Ebury Press, London.

Briggs, A (1979) *Iron Bridge to Crystal Palace*, Thames & Hudson, London.

Freeman, Allen (1979) *Railways in Britain*, Marshall Cavendish, London.

Hadfield, C (1968) *The Canal Age*, David & Charles, Newton Abbot.

Hudson, K (1976) *Archaeology of Industry*, Bodley Head, London.

de Marc, Eric (1975 edn) *Bridges of Britain*, Batsford, London.

Local history
Anderson, M D (1967) *History by the Highway*, Faber, London.

Cameron, K (1982 edn) *English Place Names*, Batsford, London.

Ekwall, E (1960) *Concise Oxford Dictionary of English Place Names*, Oxford University Press, Oxford.

Hoskins, W G (1967) *Fieldwork in Local History*, Faber, London.

Hoskins, W G (1984) *Local History in England*, Longman, London.

Iredale, D (1974) *Local History Research*, Phillimore, Chichester.

Prosse, P (1982) *The World on your Doorstep*, McGraw-Hill, Maidenhead.

Ravensdale (1972) *History on your Doorstep*, BBC, London.

Rider, P (1983) *Local History – a Handbook*, Batsford, London.

Stephens, W B (1973) *Sources for Local History*, Manchester University Press, Manchester.

English place names: see English Place Names Society, editions, published by Cambridge University Press.

Photography
Buchannan, A (1983) *Photographing Historic Buildings*, HMSO, London.

Teaching, theory and practice
Department of Education and Science
  History in the Primary and Secondary Years (1985)
  National Curriculum History Working Group Final Report (1990)
  HMSO, London

Fairclough, J and Redsell, P (1985) *Living History – reconstructing the past with children*, English Heritage, London.

Healy, S (1974) *Ideas for Teaching History*, Batsford, London.

Hodgson, J (1987) *Education Through the Arts*, National Trust, London,

ILEA (1980) *History in the Primary School*, Learning Materials Service, London.

Ironbridge Museum (1989) *Under fives and museums*, Ironbridge Gorge Trust, Telford.

Lowe, C (1990) *School Travel Organisers' Handbook*, Hobsons, Cambridge.

Morris S (1989) *A teacher's guide to using portraits*, English Heritage, London.

Noble, P (1985) *Curriculum Planning in Primary History* (Pam TH 57), Historical Association, London.

Perry, G et al (1973) *Teacher's Handbook for Environmental Studies*, Blandford, London.

Pluckrose, H (1989) *Seen Locally*, Routledge, London.

Pluckrose, H (1984) *Look around – outside*, Heinemann, London.

Purkess, S (1986) *Into the Past*, Longman, London.

Rogers, P J (1979) *The New History – theory into practice* (Pam TH 44), Historical Association, London.

Steel, D and Taylor, L (1973) *Family History in Schools*, Phillimore, Chichester

Thomson, R (1989) *When I was young...*Franklin Watts, London

Vernacular architecture
Brunskill, R (1971) *Vernacular Architecture*, Faber, London.

Cook, O (1982) *English Cottages and Farmhouses*, Thames & Hudson, London.

Muir, R (1982) *Lost Villages of Britain*, Michael Joseph, London.

Peel, J H B (1972) *An Englishman's Home*, Cassell, London.

Taylor, C (1983) *Village and Farmstead*, George Phillip, London.

West, T (1971) *The Timberframe House*, David & Charles, Newton Abbot.

General reference
Falkins, M and Gillingham J (1979) *Historical Atlas of Britain*, Granada Publishing, London.

Freeman-Grenville, G (1979) *Atlas of British History*, Rex Collings, London.

Matthew, D (1983) *Atlas of Medieval Europe*, Phaidon Press, Oxford.

Muir, R (1984) *History from the Air*, Michael Joseph, London.

Shea, M (1981) *Maritime England*, Country Life, London.

Steinberg, S H and Evans, I (1974) *Dictionary of British History*, Edward Arnold, London.

Treharne, R and Fullard, M (1973) *Muir's Historical Atlas*, George Philip, London.

See also publications by the Automobile Association (Drive Publications): eg *Treasures of Britain* (1968) and *Guide to Britain's Coast* (1984); and booklets published by Shire Publications, Cromwell House, Church Street, Princes Risborough, Buckinghamshire HP17 9AJ.

Computer Software (Humanities)
Tressell Publications, 70 Grand Parade, Brighton, BN2 2JA

Tressell publish a *Family History Pack*

Films (16mm/cassette)
Central Film Library, Chalfont Grove, Gerrards Cross, Bucks SL9 8TN

Useful addresses

The Civic Trust (Edn Dept)
17 Carlton House Terrace, London SW1Y 5AW

The Council for British Archaeology (Education Officer)
The Kings Manor, York YO1 2EP

The Council for Environmental Education
c/o School for Education, University of Reading, Berks RG1 5AQ

The Countryside Commission
19–23 Albert Road, Manchester M19 2EQ

English Heritage Education Service
Keysign House, 429 Oxford Street, London W1R 2HD

Historical Association
59a Kennington Park Road, London SE11 4JH

Historic Royal Palaces, The Education Officer,
Hampton Court Palace, East Molesey, Surrey KT8 9AU

National Farmers Union (Information Division)
Agricultural House, Knightsbridge, London SW1

National Trust (Education Department)
36 Queen Anne's Gate, London SW1H 9AS

National Trust for Scotland (Education Department)
5 Charlotte Square, Edinburgh, EH2 4DU

Shire Publications,
Cromwell House, Church Street, Princes Risborough, Bucks
HP17 9AJ

Tourist publications are obtainable through regional Tourist Offices
(see Yellow Pages)

Index